# What's on the SMART TRAVEL CD-ROM

The CD-ROM included with *SMART TRAVEL* contains a variety of tools, worksheets, and demos of popular travel programs, all designed to help you take advantage of the travel resources at your fingertips when you plan your travel by computer. In addition, you'll get $15 worth of free time on CompuServe, the online service with the most travel resources.

Here are the demos you'll find on the CD:

➡ Lyric Language, a colorful multimedia program designed to teach French and Spanish to kids and their families through video, songs, and games. You may recognize characters from the popular Family Circus comic strip in this demo.

➡ PictureIt!, a language-learning program available in Spanish, French, German, and Italian. This software allows you to create flashcards and tutorials, with sound and animation, from over 500 pictures.

➡ AAA Planner, a comprehensive and popular trip planning and mapping program. This multimedia planner includes information on hotels, restaurants, and popular destinations throughout the United States.

In addition to these demos, you'll find a wide selection of travel-related shareware and other useful programs:

➡ Travel Bag, a useful, colorful program that contains the information travelers need most: hotel, airline, and auto rental information, Las Vegas hotel and show details, emergency phone numbers, and more!

➡ TRAVEL-MATE, a full-featured DOS shareware program for the frequent traveler. Features include a travel guide listing hundreds of domestic and foreign cities, frequent flyer point tracking, a personal information manager, and many other useful tools and utilities.

➡ An auto maintenance spreadsheet, a handy worksheet designed to track your car's expenses and repairs.

➡ *Belize First* electronic magazine—just one example of the free travel publications you can find online.

You'll also discover the exciting online world of CompuServe, where you can share travel information with people around the world. Included on this CD is WinCIM for Windows, a colorful, easy interface program, and $15 of online time through ZiffNet.

## System Requirements

- 386DX-33 (486DX-33 or faster recommended)
- 4MB RAM (minimum)
- 4MB available on hard drive
- SuperVGA adapter (supporting 640 X 480 resolution and 256 colors) highly recommended
- Microsoft Mouse or 100% compatible
- Microsoft Windows 3.1 or higher
- MS-DOS 3.0 or higher
- Single-speed CD-ROM drive (double-speed recommended)

# SMART TRAVEL:
## Total **Planning** on **Your** Computer

Ziff-Davis Press

**ZIFF-DAVIS PRESS**
**EMERYVILLE, CALIFORNIA**

| | |
|---|---|
| Development Editor | Kelly Green |
| Copy Editor | Stephanie Raney |
| Project Coordinator | Ami Knox |
| Cover Design and Illustration | Regan Honda |
| Book Design | Regan Honda |
| Screen Graphics Editor | Tony Jonick |
| Technical Illustration | Cherie Plumlee |
| Word Processing | Howard Blechman |
| Page Layout | Tony Jonick |
| Indexer | Kayla Sussell |

Ziff-Davis Press books are produced on a Macintosh computer system with the following applications: FrameMaker®, Microsoft® Word, QuarkXPress®, Adobe Illustrator®, Adobe Photoshop®, Adobe Streamline™, MacLink®*Plus*, Aldus® FreeHand™, Collage Plus™.

If you have comments or questions or would like to receive a free catalog, call or write:
Ziff-Davis Press
5903 Christie Avenue
Emeryville, CA 94608
1-800-688-0448

ISBN 1-56276-307-5

Manufactured in the United States of America
♻ This book is printed on paper that contains 50% total recycled fiber of which 20% is de-inked postconsumer fiber.
10 9 8 7 6 5 4 3 2 1

# Contributing Writers

*Choosing Where to Go:* Lan Sluder
*If You Decide to Fly:* Esmeralda Yu
*If You Decide to Drive:* Wayne Kawamoto
*Hotels and Resorts:* Jack E. Buttram
*International Formalities:* Patrice-Anne Rutledge
*Tips for Bargain Hunters:* Kelly Green
*Staying Close to Home:* Howard Rothman

**Ziff-Davis Press would like to thank the following people and companies for their contributions to the CD-ROM.**

*Travel Bag v. 2.0:* Jim Tolliver
*TRAVEL-MATE v.3.2:* Copyright 1991-1995 by LLOYD'S Travel
*AAA Trip Planner:* ©1994 Compton's NewMedia, Inc., ©1994 American Automobile Association, ©1993-1994 GeoSystems Global Corporation. All Rights Reserved.
The *AAA Trip Planner* is based on the AAA 1993-1994 Tour-Book® Guides and is published by arrangement with the American Automobile Association. TourBook® is a registered trademark of the American Automobile Association. GeoLocate™ is a registered trademark of GeoSystems Global Corporation.
*Picture It!:* Trademarks/owner: Picture It!®, Penton Overseas, Inc. Product names used herein are for identification purposes only and may be trademarks of their respective companies. © 1991 Penton Overseas, Inc. All right reserved.
*Lyric Language:* Trademarks/owner: Lyric Language®, Penton Overseas, Inc. Product names used herein are for identification purposes only and may be trademarks of their respective companies. © 1992 Penton Overseas, Inc. All right reserved.
©1994 Family Circus: Bil Keane, Inc./Dist. by Cowles Syndicate, Inc.

# Table of Contents

## → *Planning Travel by Computer: Easier, Faster, and Better*

A world of travel information is now as close as your computer screen. Using the global electronic resources of the Internet; commercial online services such as America Online, CompuServe, Prodigy, Apple's e-World, and Microsoft's new Network; private bulletin board services (BBSs); the multimedia magic of CD-ROM; and the off-the-shelf ease of mapping and other travel software, you can research, plan, and even book any vacation or business trip.

Better yet, the travel help available to you on your computer is likely to be fresher, more reliable, and more complete than most that you get from traditional travel guidebooks, tourist offices, hotel and tour operators, or travel agencies.

*The travel help available to you on your computer is likely to be fresher, more reliable, and more complete.*

With nothing more than a personal computer, a modem, and some basic software, you can

- → Get detailed information about a variety of destinations so you can choose where you want to go.
- → Enjoy a sneak preview of where you're going from people who actually live there or from travelers who have been there recently.
- → See full-color photographs and videos of your destination before you go.
- → Get information on the lowest air, train, and cruise fares; hotel rates; and tour prices.
- → Learn which hotels seasoned travelers prefer at your destination, in every price range.
- → Read the latest electronic editions of many travel magazines and travel guides, or access new "e-zines" on travel.
- → Find out what the weather will be like at your destination when you're there.
- → Discover the most interesting sights, restaurants, and upcoming events at your destination, including ones unknown to the average visitor.
- → If you're going by car, decide which routes to take.

➡ If you're flying, choose the same airline reservations systems used by travel agents and airline reservation agents for the best fares and most convenient schedules.

➡ Make airline, hotel, and car rental reservations electronically.

➡ Arrange to meet local people who can show you around, providing you with a richer travel experience.

➡ Through expert advice and advance information, become less a tourist and more a traveler.

➡ **_Travel information at your fingertips_**

Travelers can access online services such as Prodigy for instant travel information previously available only from books—but note the ad at the bottom of the Prodigy screen.

# *Plan Your Travel Next Door or Around the World*

Any business or leisure trip will benefit from computer-aided planning, and even the most complex trip becomes easier to handle thanks to the technologies of the 1990s.

One Australian family used computer tools and resources to plan a one year 'round-the-world trip that began in October of 1994. Kerry Farmer, her husband, David, and their two children—Justin, age 8, and Catherine, age 6—set out from Sydney to visit more than 20 countries. Their destinations included the United States—with stops in Hawaii, Seattle, New Orleans, Orlando, Washington, Boston, and elsewhere—Canada, England and other parts of the United Kingdom, France, Italy, Austria, Hungary, the Czech Republic, Slovakia, possibly Poland, Germany, Greece, Turkey, Israel, Russia, Zimbabwe, Japan, Hong Kong, China, and Thailand.

The Farmers's trip totaled well over 30,000 air miles on a wide variety of airlines. Planning it was, according to Kerry, virtually a full-time job for several months. On a previous 'round-the-world trip in the 1980s, the Farmers had depended on what they read in guidebooks and primarily had tourist offices book hotels. This time, computers played a big role in the process, with itineraries suggested and fine-tuned by travelers met online, and hotel and other reservations made electronically.

Kerry says she followed several travel-related forums on CompuServe daily during the planning stage of the trip. She and her husband visited CompuServe's Travel Forum, U.K. Forum, and Florida Forum, among others.

"The most valuable thing has been the people we've made contact with," says Kerry. "A travel agent in Hawaii we ran into online has handled the bookings of hotels and inter-island fares more cheaply than our local travel agent could. We've made friends through the forums with people who have made phone calls, sent info, and so on, some of whom we'll be meeting up with or even staying with. This will give more personal insights into the areas we're visiting. Someone has offered to book the hotels for us in Zimbabwe. Another family we met online is also doing a RTW ('round-the-world trip). We're going to meet up with them and probably stay with them in Italy."

The Farmers travel with a Compaq Concerto 486 notebook. Says Kerry: "Our kids will be keeping e-mail contact with other children at their school and with kids we've met online. Our parents have joined CompuServe so we can communicate by e-mail while we travel.

"We're using the computer as our main form of information storage—everything from budgets to itinerary to names and addresses of friends, and records of the kids' schooling progress."

The most useful thing about trip planning by computer, according to Kerry, was that "we didn't need to take a package holiday. We could get up-to-date info from people who live in the countries so we could put together the itinerary we wanted. For a trip as long as ours, that has taken a lot of input," she says.

Even a one-city business trip can turn out better with a little help gleaned from a computer. "My trip to Seattle in 1993 was based partly on the information I got from a travel newsgroup on the Internet," says Lani Teshima-Miller. "For example, I'd read about the Underground Tour in Seattle, but when a few people there raved about it, I knew I should really check it out. What I think is the greatest thing about going online is that I hear criticisms and personal experiences…It's nice to get personal comments."

## Advantages to Travel Planning by Computer

Planning your travel by computer has a number of advantages over the traditional ways of planning a trip.

**Get more timely information**: Due to the lag time between research and publication, traditional guidebooks are often a year or even two out of date by the time they hit the bookstores. Magazine travel articles, assigned months or even years before the issue in which they actually appear comes out, have the same problem. But much of the information from online travel forums is as fresh as this morning's biscuits—with luck, your question may be answered from anywhere on the globe literally minutes after you post it. Information in travel databases may be updated daily or weekly.

**Get the scoop at ground level**: Even the best travel agent can only be an expert on a few travel subjects; many agents are glorified order takers who have

### *Travel magazines online*

Travelers can find electronic editions of travel-related magazines on-line—this one, Backpacker, The Magazine of Wilderness Travel, is in the Newsstand section of America Online.

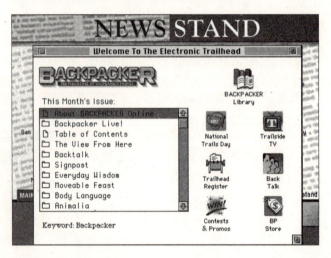

done little traveling themselves. With your computer, however, you have potential access—through online services, the Internet, and private bulletin boards—to millions of people living or traveling in every corner of the world. While few of them may be absolute experts on your destination, the combined wisdom of many residents and travelers can provide invaluable ground-zero information.

**Get the real facts, good or bad**: Airlines, hotels, tour organizers, travel agents, government tourism promotion agencies, and other travel vendors have vested financial interests in calling every destination a picture postcard, every beach a glorious golden sandy paradise with crystal-clear water, every hotel room a palace. Even some travel writers may be reluctant to provide full disclosure, for fear of libel suits or in gratitude for freebie rooms, grub, and booze. Real-world travelers, in the privacy of e-mail or in the comfort of a familiar forum, may be willing to tell you about the cockroaches in the bath or the crime on the beach.

**Get it your way**: With your PC, you control how much time, effort, and money you choose to devote to planning your next trip. Some travelers spend more time planning a trip than they spend on the trip itself, while others dip into a database here, raid a forum there, and make a quick decision. It's up to you.

### See photos of your destination—on your computer!
Photos of travel destinations, such as this one of a Swiss rail car by Max Wyss from the Photo Library of the Travel Forum on Compu-Serve, are available for downloading from several travel forums. (*Photo copyright Max Wyss.*)

You need not do it all by computer, of course. Many veteran travelers use electronic resources as just one tool of many in their travel planning. You may, for example, use Eaasy Sabre or another online reservations service to check air, hotel, or car availability and pricing, but have a local travel agent actually do the booking. Or, you may find that comments from travelers are a useful reality check to, but not a replacement for, a full-fledged guide to your destination.

Take a look at the CD-ROM accompanying this book to discover the wealth of useful travel information at your fingertips. You'll find samples of multimedia travel programs, travel-planning shareware that you can download and use immediately, a spreadsheet to help you track your auto maintenance, a travel "e-zine" (electronic magazine), and more! Further, you'll find your connection to the online world through CompuServe, one of the greatest sources of local and international travel information. Bon Voyage!

# 1

# *Choosing Where to Go*

# Technology may be shrinking the globe,

but for the traveler it's still a big, exciting world to explore: more than 200 countries and territorial entities, 58 million square miles, 21 oceans and seas, 100 major rivers, 90 mountains with a height of at least 4 miles, and 6 billion people.

For some, the biggest question about travel is "Where should I go next?" The answer to that, of course, requires some pragmatism as well as a computer. If you have only a few days of vacation, that trip to the Amazon bush will have to wait; if you have only a few *sous* in your purse, the casinos of Monte Carlo or the lights of Paris are probably out.

Regardless of the size or length of the trip you're planning, there are a variety of computer resources at your disposal to help you decide where to go: commercial online services, private bulletin boards (BBSs), the Internet, travel-related databases, reservations services, and travel-related software and multimedia products.

Assuming that you have at least a general idea of where you want to go—beaches, mountains, museums, Mayan ruins—your first stop on the info auto-bahn probably should be one or several of the online services or the Internet. Here, you can find gigabytes of travel information plus tens of thousands of in-veterate travelers, most of whom delight in giving advice.

Travel forums, in particular, are exciting and valuable electronic meeting places for travelers, travel writers, travel vendors, and anyone else who's interested in travel. If you leave a message about travel on one of these forums, you may get responses from someone who lives or works where you're heading. All of the commercial online services have at least one, and in some cases several, travel-related forums; those on CompuServe, Prodigy, and America Online are the most popular.

## ➜ *Travel Q & A on the CompuServe Travel Forum*

Here's a sample of a recent series of questions and answers posted on the Travel Forum on CompuServe (edited for brevity).

"We're looking for an island in the Caribbean where we can dive and hike and not bump into a lot of people. We're active, outdoor people and don't really care about nightlife and casinos. Any ideas where we should go?" asks a traveler from Ohio.

The answer: "If you like scuba, you'll love Saba. The island has fewer than 100 hotel rooms and no real beaches, but the diving is fabulous—and will be for a long time, thanks to Saba Marine Park. Hiking? Saba makes San Francisco look flat as a pancake, so everywhere you go is a work-out. Plus, by Caribbean standards, it doesn't cost an arm and a leg. I rented a two-bedroom Saban cottage with a pool for about $700 a week. If Saba only had some really good restaurants, it'd be paradise. Check the Forum libraries for files on Saba—we have several—and also look there for the 'Island Profiles,' one of which is on Saba."

"I live to eat—so, where should I go where the eating is great?" asks a woman from California.

"New Orleans," suggests an online ex-New Orleanian. "And here are the restaurants I'd recommend: The classics are Galatoire's, on Bourbon but not of it, maybe not quite the best, but the most New Orleans of all…. Commander's, Arnaud's, Mosca's, Antoine's, Mister B's (not old but already a classic). Some of the hot new places: Emeril's, Bayona, Irene's. Plain and simple, mouth watering, too: Bon Ton, Casamento's (a paradise of tile ceilings and delicious oyster and shrimp loaves), Mother's for debris po'boys, Central Grocery for the wonderful smell of Italian groceries and muffalettas. Burgers? The Camellia Grill, the Clover Grill (where they cook your burger under a hub cap), or Port of Call. For steak New Orleans-style and a little politics on the side, the near-original Ruth's Chris on Broad. For coffee, P.J.'s. There are a million more."

> ### → Travel Q & A on the CompuServe Travel Forum
>
> A mom queries: "What is there to do for kids in Toronto?"
>
> A traveling dad responds: "Lots for kids to do in Toronto, especially if you come in summer. Ontario Place and the Ontario Science Centre and the Metro Zoo top the list, but there's Jays games (if you can get tickets), the Toronto Islands of course, and Canada's Wonderland. The Puppet Centre and the Toronto Stock Exchange are two favorites of my kids."

## Commercial Online Services

Let's look first at the major commercial online services and what they offer, or don't offer, the prospective traveler.

To use any of these services, you'll need a personal computer (either a Mac or a PC with DOS or Windows) with a minimum of 2 to 4 megabytes of RAM (random-access memory), depending on the online service. It's desirable to have a hard drive. A modem is a must, ideally one that transmits data at 9,600 bits per second (bps) or faster. In most cases, you'll also need a major credit card for billing, or agree to have the charges automatically deducted from your checking account.

Here's how to sign up for any of these services:

1. Call the toll-free number shown below and ask for a membership kit. Be sure to ask about special introductory deals, as the online business is competitive and most services offer a free or discounted package for new members. These packages typically include several free hours of trial on-line time. The service will mail you a membership kit, which will include an ID number, password, and in most cases, disks containing proprietary software you'll need to access the service. (You may also get access software bundled with modems, new computers, or other hardware and software.) Prodigy, America Online, and e-World can only be accessed by special software provided by the services. CompuServe, while it has proprietary software, can also be accessed with generic communications

software such as White Knight or MicroPhone. Other services can also be accessed by generic communications software.

**2.** Install the software and set up your modem based on instructions in the service's manual or information materials.

**3.** Connect by calling an access number. In many cities, the services have local numbers, either their own lines or ones provided by a data service such as SprintNet. The standard now is 9,600 bps, with 14.4 and higher becoming standard in larger metropolitan areas. If you live in a remote area or anywhere outside the United States and Canada, you may have to call long distance or dial an 800 number (the call may be free but you'll pay a premium to the online service for using the toll-free number).

Charges for online access are in flux, with rate plans and rates changing almost monthly. In general, prices are going down. For example, in late 1994, Prodigy slashed its average hourly rate by about a third to $2.95 an hour, and America Online followed suit. CompuServe, e-World, and other services also have cut rates to maintain their competitiveness. Several online networks, including CompuServe, offer a basic package of services for a flat monthly fee (CompuServe's is $8.95). This includes 30 or 40 basic features such as news, airline reservations, and reference sources. Forum access and other services are charged on an hourly rate, and there may be additional surcharges for premium features such as reference databases.

## *CompuServe is viewed by some as the stodgiest of the services and by others as the savvy giant with a surprising amount of innovation*

Here's what you'll find on some of the most popular commercial online services. *CompuServe* (toll-free in the U.S. and Canada, 800-848-8990), a unit of H&R Block (the tax people), is the world's largest commercial online service, with more members than any other service, and with more local nodes in more places around the world, including the United States, Canada, Europe, Asia, and the South Pacific. A highly profitable service—H&R Block estimated CompuServe's pre-tax earnings to be more than $102 million for the fiscal year ending April 30, 1994—

CompuServe is viewed by some as the stodgiest of the services and by others as the savvy giant with a surprising amount of innovation. CompuServe is usually acknowledged as the industry leader in the variety and depth of its forums, which cover everything from a wide array of professional areas—law, medicine, aviation, journalism, public relations, investing, international trading, and more—to computers and hobbies such as gardening, pets, and a wide range of travel-related subjects and destinations.

The network is favored by many onliners with serious addictions to forums, because it is one of the few services with navigator programs to automate forum access. These programs allow members to log on, get and send messages on one or several forums, and then log off to read their messages on their own time, all automatically and quickly. This saves time and money over "live" access typical of America Online, Prodigy, e-World, and some other online services that require the user to do everyting online.

The Columbus, Ohio–based service also has extensive travel-related databases, including resources for hotels and bed and breakfasts, travel-related magazine and newspaper articles, and more.

CompuServe also offers all three online airline reservation and information systems that are available to the general public: Eaasy Sabre from American Airlines; Travelshopper, operated by Worldspan, a joint venture of Northwest, Delta, and TWA; and Official Airline Guide (OAG), a publisher of airline and other travel information. These three systems offer the same data travel agents use, but the user interface is different. All three are updated in near-real time with the latest fares and schedules from most of the world's airlines. Not included are mall commuter airlines outside the United States and airlines such as Southwest that decline to pay a fee to appear on the system.

CompuServe gives travelers more travel-related forums and information than any other service. Its offerings include the following:

> ➜ Access to the Main Travel Forum, probably the most active forum of its kind in the world, with more than 30,000 messages a month on travel and some 700,000 messages posted since its founding. Its volunteer sysops (short for *system operators*) are located around the world—one in Hong Kong, one in Switzerland, one in Canada, and several in all parts

**The official logo of the Travel Forum on CompuServe**

of the United States, including Hawaii—and members have logged on from more than 85 countries. The forum is divided into 24 sections; some of the sections are centered around specific geographic areas, and many others on a wide variety of subjects—for example, the travel writing forum, which attracts many travel writers and guidebook publishers; sections on casinos and gaming; sports travel; and private sections for travel agents and other travel professionals. CompuServe's electronic library contains more than 4,200 first-person trip reports, along with many travel-related photos in GIF, JPEG, and other formats. Among the most popular library files are items on car, hotel, and other discounts and CompuServe's collection of "hotel postcards," candid, first-person reviews of more than 1,000 hotels around the world, all filed by CompuServe members.

Access to 14 other travel-related forums, including Pacific Forum (devoted to life and travel in Australia, New Zealand, and the South Pacific), California Forum, Florida Forum (which has a very active Disney section), Japan Forum, Hong Kong Forum, UK Forum, TrainNet Forum (for rail fans and others with an interest in travel by rail), European Rail Forum, Scuba Forum, Adventure in Travel Forum, West Coast Travel Forum (covering the 13 Western U.S. states), Recreational Vehicle

Forum, Lanier Inn Forum (devoted to bed and breakfasts; includes a B&B database), and Travel Software Support Forum. CompuServe is planning to start other travel-related forums, including one that will provide members with travel information from U.S. and foreign tourist bureaus. Most forums, except some software support forums, are charged at hourly access rates.

➜ Access at no extra charge under CompuServe's basic services to Eaasy Sabre and Travelshopper reservations services (OAG is accessible with a surcharge); travel weather reports; the U.K. Automobile Association traffic and road reports; Travel Britain online; Zagat Restaurant Guides; U.S. Department of State advisories; and other travel-related services.

➜ Access, usually at surcharged rates, to millions of magazines and newspaper articles, including many on travel destinations, via databases and research gateways such as Magazine Database Plus, I-Quest, Knowledge Index, Newspaper Archives, and others.

➜ Hotel information from ABC Worldwide Hotel Guide, Lanier's Bed & Breakfast database, and other databases (see Chapter 4).

## CompuServe Pros and Cons

### Pros

◯ The most travel-related information of any commercial online service

◯ At least 15 active travel forums

◯ A large international membership, with millions of users across the United States and Canada as well as in Europe, Asia, the South Pacific, Africa, the Middle East, and Latin America

◯ Many travel-related databases

◯ Unlimited access at no extra charge to Eaasy Sabre and Travelshopper reservation systems

◯ Availability of proven graphical systems to automate forum access—popular programs include OZ-CIS, TAPCIS, Navigator for the Mac, CIS/Nav, and others

**An example of the library files available on the CompuServe Travel Forum**

| | Filename | Title | Submitted | Size | Accesses |
|---|---|---|---|---|---|
| | SAVE.CAR | Save on Car Rentals: Special Travsig d... | 11/5/94 | 21.5K | 7104 |
| | HOTEL.SAV | Hotel Discounts: Travsig membership... | 11/5/94 | 40K | 5605 |
| | COMPRS.DOC | Generic information about compresse... | 11/2/94 | 19.5K | 19 |
| | TRA12.CAT | Index of Travel Forum Data Library F... | 11/1/94 | 242.5K | 65 |
| | LIB-01.CAT | Master listing: Library 1 files. As of... | 11/1/94 | 17.5K | 183 |
| | MEGAED.ZIP | MegaEdit text Editor ver 2.11 for lar... | 10/31/94 | 134.5K | 2 |
| | AUDUBN.TXT | Audubon Tours and Workshops | 10/30/94 | 13.5K | 17 |
| | GIFSYC.NEW | Description of the Travel Forum Sca... | 10/25/94 | 7383 | 37 |
| | TRIP.MAK | TripMaker Press Release 8/23/94 | 10/11/94 | 5012 | 31 |
| | TDEMO.ZIP | TripMaker Self-Running Demo | 9/29/94 | 491.5K | 33 |
| | HMLOGO.GIF | new hmi logo test file | 9/29/94 | 6096 | 7698 |
| | MONEY.SAV | SAVE MONEY: Freebies, Discounts for... | 9/24/94 | 23.5K | 1805 |
| | HOTEL.RES | How to Make the Most Effective Hotel ... | 9/22/94 | 8787 | 529 |

(Browsing "General Interest [1]")

## Cons

◑ A premium pricing philosophy, with hourly rates higher than other services—though this may be partially or completely offset by the use of automated access programs.

◑ Somewhat more cumbersome access software—CompuServe's basic access software, CompuServe Information Manager (versions are available for Windows, DOS, and Mac) is somewhat less easy to use than that of America Online, e-World, and Prodigy, and it does not exploit the graphical, multimedia interface to its fullest potential.

◑ Limited (though improving) access to the Internet, especially compared with Delphi and America Online—access beyond present e-mail and Usenet newsgroups is promised.

**TIP**

## ➜ *Mind Your Online Manners*

Whether you visit a commercial service, private bulletin board, or the Internet seeking travel information, proper "netiquette," or electronic manners, should be part of your online personality. Here are tips to avoid getting flamed and to get the most from the information out there.

➜ Politeness counts even more online than it does in person or by phone, as the electronic medium is without the nuances of expression and tone of voice. Use emoticons such as :-) or <g> to show you're friendly, even if you're making a strong statement.

➜ Look around a bit before you start flinging out comments and questions. Listen first, then talk.

➜ Be as complete and specific as you can with your queries. Telegraphic statements such as "Tell me everything you know about France" are likely to elicit few replies.

➜ Be sure you're in the right place. The Internet's newsgroups and mailing lists are quite specific in their geographic areas and other coverage, and commercial online services are equally focused. Don't ask a question about Alaska on a newsgroup devoted to travel in Europe.

➜ Don't be a "sig raider"—someone who visits a forum asking for information but never offers any in return.

*America Online* (800-827-6364) of late has been the fastest growing online service, at least in North America. Trendy and youthful (MTV is one of its information providers), and with a colorful, easy-to-take interface, AOL came from behind to become a major force in the online world, especially in the United States. AOL has the second largest number of subscribers.

Here's some of what America Online offers travelers:

➜ The AOL travel area offers an increasing number of services for travelers, including a travel forum where more than 50,000 messages have been

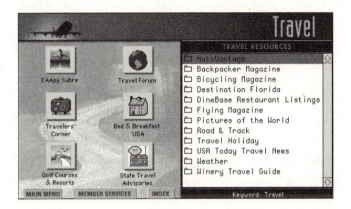

**The opening screen of the Travel Forum on America Online**

posted; a related travel library contains some 300 files; a travel guide and database to wine regions of the world; online editions of *Travel Holiday, Backpacker, Bicycling, Travel and Leisure,* and *USA Today Travel News* magazines; travel weather reports; an extensive database of award-winning restaurants; an online travel bookstore; Bed & Breakfast USA (a database of bed and breakfasts); U.S. Department of State advisories, and more.

AOL offers access to Eaasy Sabre at regular AOL hourly rates.

## Pros and Cons of America Online

### Pros

- Friendly, intuitive, and multimedia-oriented interface
- Competitive pricing—under $3 an hour at up to 9,600 bps
- Well-organized travel area with many travel services and databases in one place
- Good Internet access, including e-mail, Usenet newsgroups, WAIS and Gopher access, and ftp (file transfer protocol) ability; a Mosaic-style interface to the World Wide Web is promised for 1995

## Cons

- No automated access programs—everything must be done online
- Somewhat clunky forum software, which discourages quick browsing of messages in several sections
- Main travel forum, while increasing in activity, is less active than those on CompuServe and Prodigy
- Due to rapid system growth, members report reccurring problems with busy access nodes and other system access problems

---

 ### Finding travel info through America Online

A typical screen listing travel messages, in this case messages about Europe, on America Online's Travel Forum

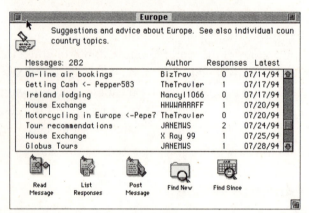

---

*Prodigy* (800-776-0836) is the child of a marriage between Sears and IBM. Once the dominant consumer online service, luring members with a low-cost flat-fee pricing system, Prodigy raised rates in 1993 and moved to an hourly pricing system in an effort to become profitable. Since then, although financial performance has improved, membership growth has slowed, and activity on its forums has declined dramatically. It is now third among the major services in number of actual subscribers, although the company itself counts users according to primary membership IDs, each allowing up to five different users. Prodigy is fighting to recover market share with aggressive price cuts, software revamps, and expanded services. It remains the only online service to require members to view advertising on most screens. In late 1994, however, Prodigy removed advertising from screens once the user is in a forum area.

 ### *A look at Prodigy's Travel Area*

Here's a look at what Prodigy offers travelers:

- The active Travel Forum, ably managed by Jack Adler, has many long-time regulars; in 1994 the forum was number 40 on *Boardwatch* magazine's list of top 100 BBSs; however, the Prodigy Travel Forum has no permanent libraries of member files as do CompuServe, America Online, and some other services.

- A wide array of other travel information is available, including city and regional guides, specialty guides, cruise information, and dining guides.

- Prodigy provides access to Eaasy Sabre at regular hourly rates.

### *Pros and Cons of Prodigy*

#### Pros

- ♌ Easy-to-use interface
- ♌ Popular Travel Forum
- ♌ Many travel databases, including several unique to Prodigy
- ♌ Competitive pricing, at under $3 an hour for access at up to 14,400 bps
- ♌ First commercial service to make available an Internet Web browser, a popular feature introduced by Prodigy in January 1995 for Windows users only.

#### Cons

- ♋ Screens carry advertising messages
- ♋ Despite new high-speed access, the graphical system can be slow
- ♋ Only limited automated programs available, and only for DOS

*Delphi* (800-695-4005), a unit of Rupert Murdoch's News Corporation, has put most of its effort into its Internet gateway. At present Delphi offers a fuller gateway than any other service.

Here's what Delphi offers travelers:

- ➡ Several travel-oriented forums
- ➡ One of the most complete Internet gateways of any commercial online service
- ➡ Access to Eaasy Sabre and Travelshopper reservation systems under basic services; access to Official Airline Guide (OAG) at surcharged rates

### *Pros and Cons of Delphi*

#### Pros

- ♌ Good Internet access

### Cons

◗ Relatively small membership base with little activity on Delphi travel-related forums

◗ Difficult interface with limited automated access

*e-World* (800-775-4556) is Apple's belated entry in the online wars. It sports an AOL-style multimedia interface—highly intuitive and excellent graphics. At present, e-World is available only for Macs and primarily in North America, but Apple says it plans a Windows interface and is expanding into Europe.

## The opening screen of e-World's Travel section

Here's what e-World offers travelers:

➡ Travel Forum, which is not very active and which has no member libraries

➡ A variety of travel databases, including the Bed & Breakfast USA service; Traveler's Edge, a collection of destination and other travel information; Fodor's Worldview service; a library of professionally written travel articles from Knight Ridder/Tribune Information Services files; and other databases

## Pros and Cons of e-World

### Pros

- Intuitive, easy-to-use interface
- Growing collection of travel databases
- Access to Eaasy Sabre at regular rates

### Cons

- Service is presently limited to Mac users
- Has at present a small membership base with little activity on the Travel Forum
- Does not offer Internet access

GEnie (800-638-9636), despite being owned by industrial giant General Electric, has never been much of a player in the online world, at least on the consumer level. While some users are fanatically loyal, GEnie is known for its tricky interface, which is difficult for newcomers. GEnie has been slipping in the membership race and now has only a fraction of the users of the major services.

Here's what GEnie offers travelers:

- Several travel-related forums, including a general Travel Forum, Florida Forum, Germany Forum, and Scuba Forum; each forum has libraries of files uploaded by members
- Some travel-related databases, including magazine articles and hotel information
- Access to Eaasy Sabre reservations service at basic rates; access to Official Airline Guide (OAG) at surcharged rates

## Pros and Cons of GEnie

### Pros

- Automated programs available for both DOS and Macintosh platforms

### Cons

- ↻ Small membership base
- ↻ Travel-related forums have little activity
- ↻ Difficult-to-use interface
- ↻ At present, no access to the Internet

*Microsoft Network* is, as of this writing, only a gleam in Bill Gates's eye: Windows 95, due out in August 1995, will have Network online software built in. Company announcements and industry gossip suggest that the service will be similar to existing services, with a highly graphical interface. It likely will have travel databases and one or more travel forums. Reportedly, Network will emphasize getting publishers and other vendors to put information on the system by paying them more to do it than do existing services. Since it is expected that Network will ship with every Windows operating system, competitors are viewing it as the new 800-pound gorilla.

## Private Bulletin Boards

There may be as many as 60,000 private BBSs in the United States alone. Many of these offer at least some travel-related information, and a number are focused entirely on travel. Marcus Endicott, author of *The Electronic Traveler: Directory of Tourism Information Sources*, a self-published guide to online travel-related services ($50 from M.L. Endicott, P.O. Box 20837, Saint Simons Island, Georgia 31522), reports that as of mid-1994, there were more than 40 travel BBSs operating in the United States, including ones focusing on Alaska, New Hampshire, Colorado, and Hawaii (see Chapters 5 and 6 for some of the best).

## The Internet

Although the exact number of Internet users is in dispute—some observers think they are exaggerated—the Internet may be used by 10 to 20 million people or more around the world, and that number is growing by at least 30,000 each month.

For the traveler, the Internet is an electronic Library of Congress of facts, figures, and people. Much of this data is difficult to fathom, and in some ways the Internet does not offer as much travel information as its hype might suggest. For example, as of this writing, there is no direct Internet access to Eaasy Sabre, Travelshopper, or OAG reservation services, but Internet users can access the systems on the commercial online services via Telnet. Telnet, however, requires full Internet access.

You can get your own access to the Internet via one of the commercial online services (in most cases this is less than full access), via a private BBS, or from a vendor specializing in Internet connections, such as Cerf.Net or Bix. In late 1994, MCI Communications Corp.announced its intent to become a large-scale Internet provider, offering a broad range of services that the company says could add millions of new users to the global network. Other large telecommunications companies may follow suit.

Costs for Internet access can range from a few dollars a month to $100 a month, depending on type of account, level of access, and other factors. Students and faculty at colleges and many employees of corporations can get access to the Internet at nominal rates through their university or corporation. There are also an increasing number of Freenets, public gateways to the Internet paid for by state or local tax dollars.

***America Online: Expanded but incomplete Internet access***

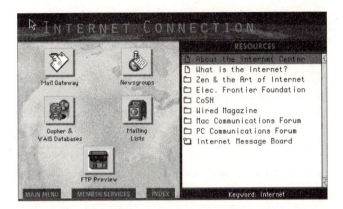

At least four areas are of special interest to travelers with Internet access:

| Usenet Newsgroups | Newsgroups are the Internet equivalent of commercial online forums or private bulletin boards, and those in the travel area tend to cover the same ground. Surprisingly, most are not nearly as active as similar forums on CompuServe or Prodigy in terms of postings and replies. Further, much of the activity on the Internet is conducted via private e-mail, which leaves forum watchers with less public information. Some of the more active Internet travel-related newsgroups include bit.listserv.travel-l, rec.travel.Europe, rec.travel.usa-canada, rec.travel.asia, rec.travel.air, rec.travel.cruise, rec.travel.marketplace, and rec.travel.misc (which is a mish-mash of everything not covered in the other rec.travel groups). Despite the size of the Internet, none of these Usenet newsgroups usually gets more than 200 or 300 messages posted a day, a considerably lower rate of activity than several of the commercial services. Some of the soc. groups may also be of interest to travelers. For example, soc.culture.latin-america would be valuable to those traveling to South America. |
| --- | --- |

| Mailing Lists | This is a feature of the Internet that may appeal to those who have a great interest in travel to a specific location. A *mailing list* is an Internet bulletin board on a single highly focused theme. For example, the New Orleans mailing list, moderated by Ed Branley, a New Orleans native, has many New Orleans fans, residents, and ex-residents on board. Usually there are 20 or 30 messages a day about New Orleans. Recent message threads discussed and listed the best and worst movies made in New Orleans, the ten best places to get a hamburger in the Crescent City, and a collection of recipes for red beans and rice, a favorite local dish. There are at least six mailing lists about San Francisco, 13 about New York, 14 on Russia, and 20 on the U.K. |
|---|---|
| Archives | Several places on the Internet are storage sites, or *archives*, for travel information. Travel archives include ftp.cc.umanitoba.ca, which can be reached using ftp. Searching Internet resources using Gopher, WAIS, Archie, Webcrawler, or other search tools will also elicit lots of travel information. |
| World Wide Web Sites | With the increasing commercialization of the Internet, travel vendors are developing their own sites on the Web. Pages here can feature elaborate multimedia presentations, including fancy hypertext, graphics, and video. Getting to and benefiting from the Web sites, however, is limited to those who have relatively full Internet access and Mosaic, Netscape, or other similar software. |

## Travel-Related Multimedia and Software

The Sierra Club, National Geographic, and an increasing number of private publishers produce CD-ROM travel titles for Windows and Macintosh, covering everything from the Taj Mahal to the Trans-Siberian Railway to Mt. Everest. Compton's is the biggest CD-ROM publisher, producing titles on a wide range of subjects besides travel.

Travel-related software can be valuable once you've made a decision on your destination and are looking for more information. Two products recommended by travel bookstore owner Bryan Smith, who operates Bon Voyage! in Fresno,

California, are *Magnificent Rocky, a Guide to Rocky Mountains National Park*, with excellent photographs and video narrated by park rangers (under $30); and *Let's Go Europe*, with maps, photos, video, text, spoken phrases, hotels, and restaurants (around $40). Of the latter, Smith says that it is "pretty well done, but you still need the *Let's Go* book."

Other hot products include mapping software (see Chapter 3), programs that teach a foreign language (see Chapter 5), and specialized programs that help manage travel expenses or frequent flyer mileage. (Some travelers use simple accounting programs such as Quicken to handle these tasks, substituting mileage points for dollars or using travel expense categories instead of the usual accounting categories.)

Demand so far has been limited by the relatively high cost for a product that only covers a single destination, and the difficulty of carrying a computer with a CD-ROM player on a trip. But with the production of more comprehensive travel titles, demand is sure to increase.

A much cheaper software route is travel software, which costs nothing more than a minimal registration fee should you choose to keep it. You can download many shareware travel programs from the online services, and a few examples— Travel Bag and TRAVEL-MATE— are included on the CD-ROM accompanying this book. Keep in mind that shareware programs are designed to be simple and useful; you'll find no bells and whistles here.

**Lan Sluder** is a travel writer and travel magazine publisher. He edits and publishes *Belize First* , a quarterly magazine on travel and life in Belize with both traditional and e-zine editions; see the CD-ROM accompanying this book for a sample issue. His travel articles have appeared in the *Chicago Tribune*, the *Miami Herald*, *Caribbean Travel and Life*, the *New York Times*, and elsewhere. Active on the Internet and several commercial online systems, he is a volunteer sysop on the Travel Forum on CompuServe.

# 2

## *If You Decide to Fly*

**If** you decide to fly to your destination, you can easily reserve your flight from your computer using an online reservation system. Each of the three largest online service providers offers a gateway to the Eaasy Sabre system, created by American Airlines. Eaasy Sabre is the airline reservations system used by travel agents around the world. Not only can you make reservations for both domestic and international flights, but you can also make hotel and car reservations through Eaasy Sabre. This popular service provides you with an efficient way to make all of your travel arrangements.

In addition to Eaasy Sabre, some online providers offer a gateway to two other services that allow you to make flight reservations: Worldspan Travelshopper and Official Airline Guide (OAG). Of the three services, OAG is the most comprehensive travel planning tool; it gives the user access to databases containing information on tours, cruises, discount travel packages, U.S. State Department Advisories, arrival and departure schedules for several U.S. airports, and more (see Chapter 5 for more details). You can also make hotel reservations using OAG. OAG is known for its accuracy as well as its breadth of coverage. In fact, according to OAG, of the 415 airlines worldwide that use automated reservations systems, 413 look to OAG for schedule data. On the down side, OAG imposes a hefty surcharge, while Worldspan Travelshopper and Eaasy Sabre do not. Worldspan Travelshopper, while it is free of charge and fairly comprehensive, has the disadvantage of not being accessible from Prodigy, America Online, and many of the smaller online services.

This chapter will deal primarily with how to use Eaasy Sabre, the most popular and most easily accessible of the reservations systems, through each of the largest online services—CompuServe, Prodigy, and America Online.

## Reservations Services Offered by Online Providers

| Online Provider | Reservations Services Provided |
| --- | --- |
| CompuServe | Eaasy Sabre, Travelshopper, OAG (with surcharge) |
| America Online | Eaasy Sabre |
| Prodigy | Eaasy Sabre |

## Reservations Services Offered by Online Providers (Continued)

| Online Provider | Reservations Services Provided |
|---|---|
| Delphi | Eaasy Sabre, Travelshopper, OAG (with surcharge) |
| e-World | Eaasy Sabre |
| GEnie | Eaasy Sabre, OAG (with surcharge) |

## What You Can Do on Eaasy Sabre

✔ Make reservations on any major airline in the world

✔ Search for the lowest fares through the Bargain Finder feature

✔ Select your preferred seat

✔ Arrange for special meals if you have certain dietary needs

✔ If you are traveling with others, make reservations for everyone in your travel group

✔ If you are a member of a particular airline's frequent flyer program, limit your search to flights on that airline

✔ After making your reservation, choose how you want your ticket delivered

✔ If you need a hotel room and a car rental, make these reservations as well

Because Eaasy Sabre is primarily an airline reservations system, the selection of hotels and car rental agencies is limited to the major hotel chains and rental companies. However, if you are a member of a frequent flyer program that allows you to accumulate mileage when you stay at certain hotels or rent from certain car rental agencies, Eaasy Sabre provides you with a quick way to make all of your travel arrangements in one shot.

In the next section, you will learn how to use Eaasy Sabre by accessing CompuServe. Please keep in mind that though we'll concentrate on CompuServe, making reservations through Eaasy Sabre is similar on the other commercial online services.

## Why use a travel agent? Your computer has all the answers.

Online reservations systems such as Eaasy Sabre and OAG give you access to the same flight information used by travel agents around the world.

# Accessing Eaasy Sabre through CompuServe

If you have the CompuServe Information Manager for Windows (WinCIM), making flight reservations has never been easier. From the Services box in WinCIM, click on the Travel icon. Select Air Information/Reservations from the Travel box menu. A box containing Eaasy Sabre options will appear. Select Access Eaasy Sabre. A faster way to access Eaasy Sabre is to simply click on the Go icon (the green light) on the WinCIM ribbon bar and type **sabrecim**.

 **Eaasy Sabre access through WinCIM**

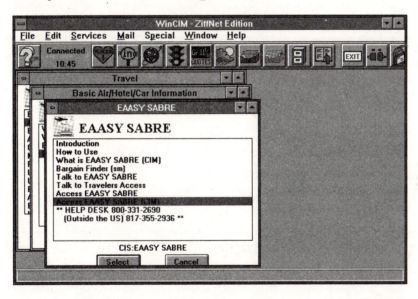

After you enter the Eaasy Sabre system, a box will pop up requesting you to input your Eaasy Sabre identification number and password. If you have an Eaasy Sabre ID number and password, simply type this information in the blanks provided. If you have never used the Eaasy Sabre system or if you have forgotten your ID number and password, you must first enroll by selecting Apply. Enrolling in Eaasy Sabre is free of charge.

To enroll in Eaasy Sabre and obtain an ID number and password (which you need to access the system), you must fill out the online application. Eaasy Sabre will ask you to enter your name, address, phone number, and a password of your choice. After you have completed the online application form, Eaasy Sabre will immediately assign you an ID number.

**TIP**

Remember to write down your ID number and password and keep these in a safe place.

After entering your ID number and password, you will see a menu with the following choices:

- ➡ Flights and Fares
- ➡ Cars
- ➡ Hotels
- ➡ Current Itinerary
- ➡ Travel Profile
- ➡ Review Reservations
- ➡ AAdvantage Program
- ➡ Change Eaasy Sabre Password
- ➡ Terms and Conditions
- ➡ About Eaasy Sabre CIM

### ➡ About Travel Profile

Before you begin making reservations, you should consider filling out your travel profile. Select Travel Profile from the menu and enter your seating preference, special dietary needs, if any, and credit card information. Doing this will allow you to speed up the reservations process. Of course, you can change your travel profile from time to time, or select a different seat from the one you specified in your travel profile when you are actually making the reservation.

Here's how to make your flight reservation. Let's say you want to fly from Los Angeles to Amsterdam on July 15, 1995, and you would like a late afternoon flight. You want to return to Los Angeles on July 30, 1995.

First, select Flights and Fares from the menu and enter your departure information.

---

➡️ ***Enter your departure information in the destination box***

```
┌─────────────────────────────────────────────────────┐
│                    Destination                        │
│                                                       │
│  Departure City or Code: lax                          │
│                    Date: 15-jul-1995  Time: 04:00pm   │
│      Arrival City or Code: ams                        │
│      Number of Passengers: 1                          │
│                                                       │
│  (Optional)                                           │
│    Airline Name or Code: _____             │
│   ┌────────┐  ┌───────┐  ┌──────────────┐  ┌────────┐ │
│   │Flights │  │ Fares │  │ Preferences  │  │ Cancel │ │
│   └────────┘  └───────┘  └──────────────┘  └────────┘ │
└─────────────────────────────────────────────────────┘
```

By the way, you do not need to know the three-letter codes for Los Angeles and Amsterdam. After you enter the name of each city, a box will pop up that shows a series of three-letter city codes next to the names of those cities. Simply click on the correct item.

After you have entered your departure information, select the Flights box. A schedule of flights from Los Angeles to Amsterdam on July 15, 1995 will appear, starting with the flight closest to your chosen time of departure.

This flight schedule above shows the following information about each scheduled flight on July 15, 1995: whether the flight is direct or stops in another city, the time of departure and arrival, the airline (represented by its two-letter airline code), the number of stops the flight will make en route to your destination, and the type of aircraft.

If you highlight a particular flight and click on the Detail box below the list of flights, you will see more detailed information regarding that flight, including the name of the airline and fare classes available on that flight.

## Find your flight quickly and easily

After you've entered your information in the destination box, pressing Flights will give you a list of scheduled flights on the day you wish to fly to your given destination (in this case, from Los Angeles to Amsterdam on July 15, 1995).

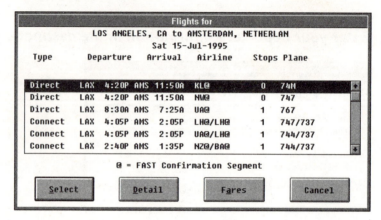

| Type | Departure | Arrival | Airline | Stops | Plane |
|------|-----------|---------|---------|-------|-------|
| Direct | LAX 4:20P | AMS 11:50A | KL@ | 0 | 74M |
| Direct | LAX 4:20P | AMS 11:50A | NW@ | 0 | 747 |
| Direct | LAX 8:30A | AMS 7:25A | UA@ | 1 | 767 |
| Connect | LAX 4:05P | AMS 2:05P | LH@/LH@ | 1 | 747/737 |
| Connect | LAX 4:05P | AMS 2:05P | UA@/LH@ | 1 | 744/737 |
| Connect | LAX 2:40P | AMS 1:35P | NZ@/BA@ | 1 | 744/737 |

Highlighting the flight and clicking on the Fares box will also show you the different fare classes available on that flight, the advance purchase requirements, and other requirements such as minimum/maximum stay.

Here's how to complete the reservation. Let's say you've decided to fly KLM from Los Angeles to Amsterdam. If you highlight that flight and click on Select, another box will appear asking if you want to add a return flight. If you indicate that you want to reserve a return flight, a box similar to the Destination box shown earlier will pop up, this time prompting you for information regarding your return date (in this example, July 30, 1995). Once you have completed this box, another schedule of flights will appear. Select your desired return flight. The procedure for selecting a return flight is the same as that for selecting a departure.

After you have added your return flight, Eaasy Sabre will display your itinerary.

At this stage, you have several options. You can confirm your itinerary, select the fare you want, get more details regarding each flight, obtain a summary, or cancel your itinerary.

### Eaasy Sabre's itinerary display

When you're done choosing your flights, Eaasy Sabre automatically displays your itinerary.

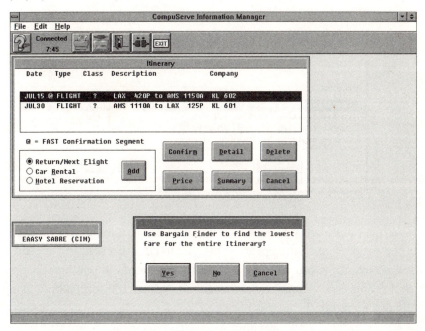

If you choose Confirm, a box will appear inquiring if you want to use the Bargain Finder feature of Eaasy Sabre to select the lowest fare for your itinerary. If you do, select Yes. A box showing the full fare and lowest available fares for your itinerary will be displayed.

Let's say you decide on the lowest available fare of $1,064.75. Highlight that fare and click on Select to confirm that you want this price. You will be shown the fare you have chosen and the rules and restrictions that apply to it. Be aware that the lowest available fares usually have restrictions on cancellations and changes as well as advance purchase requirements.

### _Eaasy Sabre's Bargain Finder_

The Bargain Finder option allows you to view the lowest available fares for your flight, along with the penalties and restrictions that apply to those fares.

| Select Bargain Finder Price | | | |
|---|---|---|---|
| Currency: USD | Fare Basis | Adult | Child |
| Full Fare | MEERT | 1494.75 | |
| Lowest Avail | BHWANEU | 1064.75 | |
| Lowest Avail/No Penalty | MEERT | 1494.75 | |
| Lowest Avail/No Adv Pur. | MHWEUPX | 1264.75 | |
| Lowest Avail/No Min-Max | MEERT | 1494.75 | |

[ Select ]        [ Cancel ]

At this point, Eaasy Sabre lets you make your seat assignment and select a special meal. A box will appear asking you to choose a seat and specify your meal preference if you have any special dietary needs. If you initially created a travel profile (see "About Travel Profile" above), such information will automatically be entered in the spaces provided.

After you have made seat and meal selections, Eaasy Sabre asks you how you want your ticket delivered. A box describing different ticket delivery options appears. You can have your ticket delivered to you via free overnight delivery or regular seven-day mail, or you can choose from several additional Eaasy Sabre options (picking up your ticket at the airline's ticket office or at an Eaasy Sabre travel agency, and so on).

**NOTE** You will need to enter your credit card information and address if you decide to have your ticket delivered to you. This information will be automatically entered if you previously created a travel profile. If you decide to pick up your ticket at an airline ticket office or a travel agent, Eaasy Sabre will not prompt you for this information.

If you decide to pick up your ticket from an airline ticket office or a travel agent, a box will appear showing your itinerary number and the last day on which you can purchase your ticket to obtain the fare you selected.

*Choosing seat and meal preference options*

```
┌──────────────────────────────────────────────────────────────┐
│                     Passenger 1 Information                    │
│ ┌Passenger: 1─────────┐         Seat Preference Options        │
│  First Name: _____         Reserve any seat          [▲]  │
│  Last Name:  _____       No smoking aisle               │
│                                 No smoking window              │
│ ┌Phone Number(s)──────┐         Smoking aisle                  │
│  Home: _____          Smoking window           [▼]  │
│  Work: _____X                                        │
│                                 Meal Preference Options        │
│ ┌Frequent Flyer Information┐    No special meal          [▲]  │
│  Airline        Freq Flyer No   Bland                          │
│  K.L.M. AIRLINES _____        Diabetic                       │
│  _____      _____         Kosher                         │
│  _____      _____         Low calorie             [▼]   │
│  _____      _____                                        │
│  _____      _____         ┌──────┐     ┌────────┐        │
│  _____      _____         │  OK  │     │ Cancel │        │
│                                 └──────┘     └────────┘        │
└──────────────────────────────────────────────────────────────┘
```

Write down your itinerary number on a piece of paper if you need to pick up your ticket from a travel agency or an airline ticket office. The agent can quickly pull up your reservation if you have this number handy.

Eaasy Sabre also lets you cancel or change your reservation at a later date. After you log onto Eaasy Sabre, a box will appear showing your departure date and itinerary number. Under the departure date and itinerary number are two options: Review and Cancel Reservation. If you wish to change your reservation, select Review and follow the instructions on the screen. If you wish to cancel, select Cancel Reservation.

**TIP**

# Accessing Eaasy Sabre through Prodigy

Making flight reservations through Prodigy is not much different from the procedure outlined above for CompuServe. Prodigy provides an easy-to-use graphical Eaasy Sabre menu. To access Eaasy Sabre through Prodigy, select Reservations

Online from the Travel Highlights Menu (or jump to EAASY SABRE). The Eaasy Sabre menu will appear, giving you six initial choices:

**1.** *Eaasy Sabre Reservations* connects you immediately to the Eaasy Sabre reservations menu.

**2.** *Ticketing Options* describes the six ticket delivery options offered by Eaasy Sabre, along with their surcharges, if any:

➡ Free overnight express delivery

➡ Saturday express delivery

➡ First-class mail (free)

➡ Pick up at one of over 400 locations throughout the United States

➡ Courier service (for last-minute reservations)

➡ "On hold" ticketing option

**3.** *Enroll in Eaasy Sabre* begins the enrollment process (if you do not have an Eaasy Sabre ID number and password).

**4.** *EAASY Tutor* is an online tutorial that explains the reservation process, acquaints you with airline and fare codes, describes how you can find the cheapest fare for your itinerary, change your itinerary or cancel it, and finally, how to pay for your tickets and have them delivered to you.

**5.** *Travel Glossary* provides you with definitions of unfamiliar terms you may encounter on Eaasy Sabre.

**6.** *Eaasy Sabre Message Center* allows you to send messages to the Eaasy Sabre Support Desk and EAASY/Quiktix Customer Service if you have any questions about reservations or ticket delivery.

~🖥~

To enroll in Eaasy Sabre through Prodigy, select the third option in the Eaasy Sabre menu shown above. Before you enroll, you must have the following information ready:

➡ A valid credit card if you intend to pay online for the tickets you reserve

➡ Seating preferences (for example, aisle or window)

### The Eaasy Sabre menu on Prodigy

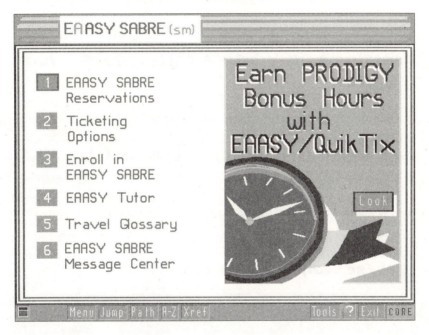

- Meal preferences (if you have special dietary needs)
- A password (four to eight characters; must be different from your Prodigy password).

If you have an American Airlines frequent flyer number and a travel agent you want to use, you can also enter these items during the enrollment process.

Once you have enrolled in Eaasy Sabre, you are ready to make your flight reservation. Select the Flight Reservations option from the Eaasy Sabre reservations menu. As on CompuServe, Eaasy Sabre on Prodigy prompts you for information regarding your departure. After you enter the departure information, you will see a list of available flights similar to the one you saw earlier for CompuServe. You can select the flight of your choice and then make a reservation for a return flight.

The Bargain Finder feature of Eaasy Sabre is also available to Prodigy users. After you have created your itinerary, you can select the lowest fare and find out the restrictions for that fare. Then, you can make your seat and meal selections and specify your ticket delivery preference.

## Accessing Eaasy Sabre through America Online

Making airline reservations through America Online is identical to the procedure outlined above for CompuServe and Prodigy. After you log onto America Online, enter the keyword EAASY SABRE. You will be prompted for your Eaasy Sabre ID number and password. If you do not have an ID number and password, fill out the online application (free of charge). You will be assigned an ID number; use this ID number to log onto Eaasy Sabre.

 **The Eaasy Sabre menu on America Online**

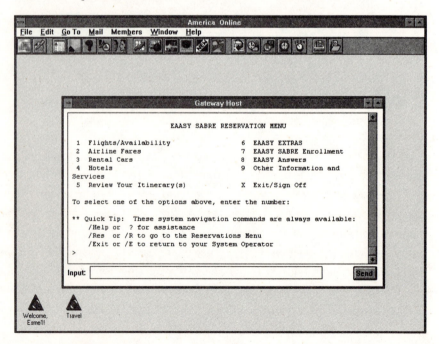

Select Flights/Availability from the Reservation menu to make your reservation, and then enter your departure information. You will see a flight schedule similar to the one shown below. You can get more details about each flight by double-clicking on its listing.

---

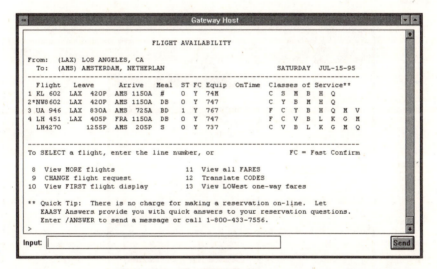

➡️ *The flight schedule on America Online*

```
─                          Gateway Host                          ▼ ▲
                                                                    ↕
                         FLIGHT AVAILABILITY

   From:  (LAX) LOS ANGELES, CA
     To:  (AMS) AMSTERDAM, NETHERLAN                 SATURDAY  JUL-15-95
   ---------------------------------------------------------------------
     Flight   Leave     Arrive    Meal  ST FC Equip  OnTime  Classes of Service**
   1 KL 602   LAX 420P  AMS 1150A  #    O  Y  74M            C  S  M  B  H  Q
   2*NW8602   LAX 420P  AMS 1150A  DB   O  Y  747            C  Y  B  M  H  Q
   3 UA 946   LAX 830A  AMS 725A   BD   1  Y  767            F  C  Y  B  H  Q  M  V
   4 LH 451   LAX 405P  FRA 1150A  DB   O  Y  747            F  C  V  B  L  K  G  M
     LH4270       1255P AMS 205P   S    O  Y  737            C  V  B  L  K  G  M  Q


   ---------------------------------------------------------------------
   To SELECT a flight, enter the line number, or          FC = Fast Confirm

    8   View MORE flights                11   View all FARES
    9   CHANGE flight request            12   Translate CODES
   10   View FIRST flight display        13   View LOWest one-way fares

   ** Quick Tip:  There is no charge for making a reservation on-line.  Let
      EAASY Answers provide you with quick answers to your reservation questions.
      Enter /ANSWER to send a message or call 1-800-433-7556.
    >                                                                   ↕
   Input: |                                                      |  Send
```

---

After you have selected a flight for your departure, you can reserve a return flight and find the lowest fare for your itinerary using Bargain Finder. You can also find the lowest fares by clicking on the Airline Fares option in the Reservation menu. Eaasy Sabre will show you a list of flights and the booking code for the fare you have chosen.

# Making Flight Reservations with Worldspan Travelshopper

Travelshopper is the consumer interface to the Worldspan reservations system, which is owned by TWA, Northwest Airlines, and Delta Airlines. You can gain access to Worldspan Travelshopper through CompuServe and selected other services.

To find Travelshopper in CompuServe, click on the Travel icon in the Services box in WinCIM. Select Air Information/Reservations from the Travel box menu, and then choose Worldspan Travelshopper(CIM). You'll notice that the Worldspan Travelshopper interface is similar to Eaasy Sabre's menus and screens.

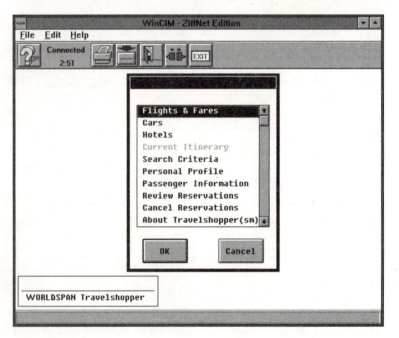

### ➜ The Worldspan Travelshopper(CIM) opening screen

To speed up the reservations process, you can complete the Search Criteria to narrow your selection of flights and create your Personal Profile. The Personal Profile allows you to enter information such as your preferred reservation class and ticketing method. Once you have entered this information, you are ready to reserve flights and check for the lowest fares.

Here's how to make your reservation with Travelshopper. Choose Flights and Fares from the Travelshopper(CIM) menu. As with Eaasy Sabre, a box will pop up prompting you to fill in your departure city, destination, date and time of arrival, and number of passengers. Click on Flights to see the flights scheduled for that day. When you select your preferred flight, another box appears that allows you to reserve a return flight. When your itinerary is complete, click on Price to obtain a list of the fares for your chosen itinerary. Highlight the fare that best suits your needs (keeping in mind the various restrictions for different fare classes) and select Reserve to reserve the highlighted fare.

If you wish to price an itinerary before reserving a flight, choose Flights and Fares from the Travelshopper (CIM) menu, enter your departure information, then click on Fares. You will see a list of available fares, their restrictions (advance purchase, minimum/maximum stay), and airline codes. If you highlight a particular fare and click on Rules, you will get a more detailed description of the restrictions that apply to that particular fare. After you have reviewed the restrictions that apply to different fares, you can choose your fare and reserve your itinerary.

As with Eaasy Sabre, you can tell Travelshopper how you want your ticket delivered to you. You can pick up your ticket at a local TWA or Northwest office, or you can purchase your tickets at the airline ticket counter. You can also have your tickets sent to a Worldspan travel agency or pay by credit card and have your tickets delivered.

**NOTE**   If you pay for your Travelshopper ticket by credit card, at least one segment of your itinerary must be on either TWA or Northwest Airlines.

## Making Flight Reservations with OAG

To access OAG (Official Airlines Guide) Electronic Edition from CompuServe, choose OAG Electronic Edition from the Air Information/Reservations menu. Then, from the OAG Travel Service box, select Access OAG Travel Service ($). OAG carries the following surcharges: $10 per hour (17 cents per minute) between 7 p.m. and 8 a.m., and $28 per hour (47 cents per minute) between 8 a.m. and 7 p.m.

OAG Electronic Edition allows you to book flights, find low fares, view actual seat availability, and arrange for ticketing. The procedure for booking a flight on OAG Electronic Edition is similar to that used for Eaasy Sabre and Worldspan

Travelshopper. You enter the departure city, destination, and preferred date and time. OAG Electronic Edition then displays flight schedules chronologically by departure time and fares from lowest to highest.

 ### The OAG opening screen

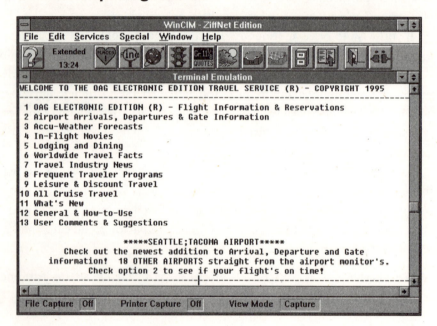

```
                      WinCIM - ZiffNet Edition
  File   Edit   Services   Special   Window   Help
 ┌───┐ Extended   ┌──┐┌──┐┌──┐┌──┐┌──┐┌──┐┌──┐┌──┐┌──┐┌──┐┌──┐
 │ ? │  13:24     │  ││  ││  ││  ││  ││  ││  ││  ││  ││  ││  │
 └───┘            └──┘└──┘└──┘└──┘└──┘└──┘└──┘└──┘└──┘└──┘└──┘
                           Terminal Emulation
WELCOME TO THE OAG ELECTRONIC EDITION TRAVEL SERVICE (R) - COPYRIGHT 1995
-------------------------------------------------------------------------

 1 OAG ELECTRONIC EDITION (R) - Flight Information & Reservations
 2 Airport Arrivals, Departures & Gate Information
 3 Accu-Weather Forecasts
 4 In-Flight Movies
 5 Lodging and Dining
 6 Worldwide Travel Facts
 7 Travel Industry News
 8 Frequent Traveler Programs
 9 Leisure & Discount Travel
10 All Cruise Travel
11 What's New
12 General & How-to-Use
13 User Comments & Suggestions


                 *****SEATTLE;TACOMA AIRPORT*****
        Check out the newest addition to Arrival, Departure and Gate
  information!  18 OTHER AIRPORTS straight from the airport monitor's.
             Check option 2 to see if your flight's on time!

 File Capture  Off     Printer Capture  Off     View Mode  Capture
```

In addition to flight information, you have access to several databases on travel news and tours, cruises, discount travel packages, frequent flyer programs, U.S. State Department Travel Advisories, hotel and dining choices, ski resorts, and actual arrival/departure information for several U.S. cities.

Making airline reservations for domestic and foreign trips has never been easier: Simply log onto Eaasy Sabre, OAG, or Travelshopper through an online service. The user-friendly menus provided by each online service will allow you to navigate these reservations systems with ease. You can select the most convenient itinerary and the lowest fares, confirm your reservation, get your ticket delivered, and change or cancel your reservation. If you don't mind paying OAG's surcharge, you can even have access to a wealth of information on tours, cruises, lodging, and dining. Bon voyage!

**Esmeralda Yu is a lawyer who loves to travel and write in her spare time. After practicing law in Los Angeles from 1988 to 1994, she moved to Amsterdam, where she now resides with her husband.**

# 3 | *If You Decide to Drive*

# Whether

you're finding the way to San Jose or just driving to the next fork in the road, your computer can help get you there. Although it can't take control of your steering wheel and drive the car for you—the technology isn't quite there yet—it can analyze the available paths between two locations, recommend routes, and print directions and a map of your chosen itinerary. It can also tell you about interesting points along the way.

To make your computer into such a helpful travel guide, you'll need trip planning software like Automap Road Atlas, Compton's AAA Trip Planner, DeLorme's Map'n'Go, or Expert's Travel Planner Gold.

But knowing how to get there isn't everything—your car has to be in shape to make the trip. You can use a PC to track your vehicle's maintenance and repairs to ensure that it's road ready. Using any spreadsheet program, such as Lotus 1-2-3, Excel, or Quattro Pro, your PC can track oil changes, tire purchases and rotations, and all repairs. Most importantly, it can tell you what that car is costing you and reveal when it's time for a thorough check-up by your mechanic.

When you get on the road and the family's enthusiasm dwindles while trekking endless miles, a portable computer in the car can also provide entertainment. Although it's hard to compete against the portable game systems—the Nintendo Gameboys and SEGA GameGears of the world—portable computers offer games that other systems don't have, and they double as a way for you and your kids to record trip memories.

This chapter will show you how your computer can work for your car.

## Getting There: Trip Planning Software

For the first leg of our journey, we'll look at trip planning software. These are specialized programs that figure out the best way to get from where you are to where you want to go. It's a digital variation on classic geometry—getting from point A to point B. (But we all know that the best way to get there is not necessarily a straight line!)

Trip planners feature digitized charts that appear on your computer's screen—electronic versions of the maps that are available at gas stations (and are impossible to fold).

In telling you how to get to point B, trip planning software considers stops you might want to make along the way. For example, on the way to your final destination, you may want to visit Aunt Hilda and Uncle Herman, who live some 30 miles from the highway. You may also know of an interesting museum that's slightly off the beaten track, and there's a scenic National Park that you want to drive through because you've heard that this is a great time of year to see the moose. No matter where you want to go or how you want to get there, your computer can consider all these side trips in planning your route.

Travel programs also estimate how long it takes to drive each leg of the trip by considering your planned speed (within legal limits, of course) and the types of roads you're driving. Finally, like an auto club or restaurant guide, the computer is your local expert on worthwhile food and fun in any given area. This way, when you get to your ultimate location you'll have things to do, and you won't be stuck sitting in your hotel room watching game shows. Travel programs provide information about points of interest and also list restaurants, with numbers to call for more information.

> *It's a digital variation on classic geometry—getting from point A to point B.*

Of course, as always you'll want to call ahead and make reservations, and calls to the tourist bureaus will reveal additional information about local festivals and activities. But your computer can perform much of the legwork to get you well on your way. There are a variety of trip planning programs on the market, and now we'll take a quick look at some of the best.

~🖳~

Compton's *AAA Trip Planner* offers basic routing, mapping, and trip planning functions, and it brings digitized AAA information to the mix. The advantage of this program is that when you're searching for food or lodging, AAA Trip Planner helps you find the right places, based on price and AAA's well-known diamond star rating system. AAA Trip Planner contains some 34,000 AAA-rated hotels, motels, lodges, resorts, restaurants, and attractions.

If you've traveled much by car, chances are you've already used AAA guides and will be right at home using the digitized version. The program also offers AAA's general information on cities and locations. You should strongly consider this one for its integrated AAA ratings and first-rate routing features.

**AAA Trip Planner: A digitized guidebook for local areas**

Even if you don't need the mapping capability, AAA Trip Planner lets you locate restaurants and lodging anywhere based on price and quality.

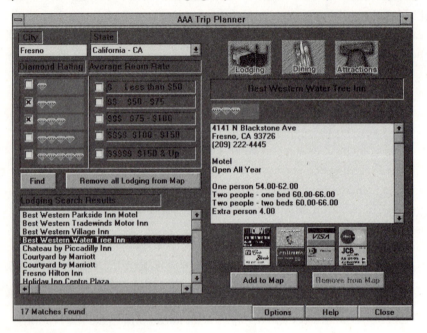

Years ago, *Automap Road Atlas* was the first product on the market to offer trip planning capabilities. This latest version offers information on states, cities, other land areas, and regional driving laws, and it also includes phone numbers for road, weather, and tourist information. Automap includes a "places of interest" command, which tells you what's worth seeing along your planned route. And it can even calculate your overall gas consumption.

Automap Road Atlas also offers add-ons. Automap's *Destination Europe* comes with some 8,400 cities and 250,000 miles of motorways, autobahns, and roads in Europe. The *Destination Ski* add-on provides information on some 590 North American ski resorts, listing size, number of runs and lifts, average snowfall, and phone numbers for more information on planning a great ski vacation.

### Automap Road Atlas helps you predict trip expenses

Automap can calculate overall fuel consumption and help you project trip expenses.

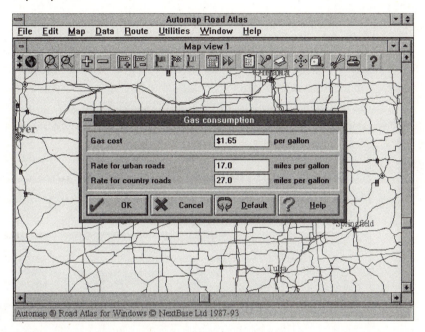

Based on more accurate mapping data from ETAK, *Automap Streets* provides precise street maps that cover 98 percent of the United States. This enhanced mapping capability lets the program locate almost any street, address, or intersection in the country; indicate one-way streets; and display latitude, longitude, and zip codes for any location.

Since the program comes on CD-ROM, you can transfer portions of the maps to a notebook computer or any hard drive. A special version of Automap Streets works directly with navigational systems such as the satellite-based global positioning system (GPS). With GPS, the program can show your exact location on the map.

The Automap Streets CD contains one free map of the county (and surrounding area) of your choice. You have to buy additional maps from the company, which will give you codes to unlock sections of the CD. Automap Streets doesn't offer the routing features of the other trip planning programs, but its maps are the most accurate ones around.

DeLorme's *Map'n'Go* offers strong routing capability, listings of points of interest within a range of your planned route, and slide shows that tell you more about a locale. Map'n'Go also comes with a full North American Road Atlas so you can look at your route on paper; or you can simply print out the maps on your screen. The program can also search for cities based on area code and zip code.

DeLorme Mapping also offers *Street Atlas USA* and *MapExpert*, both on CD-ROM. Amazingly, these CDs claim to contain every street in the United States.

 ### Map'n'Go: Find your way by zip code or area code

Map 'n' Go can locate regions based on area code or zip code, and then tell you all the sights to see there.

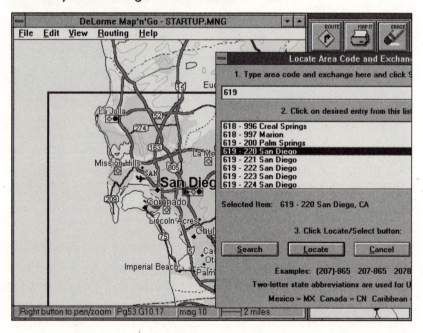

Both products use the same maps and can find locations by name, area, or zip code. Street Atlas USA lets you view the maps and export them to other Windows applications, while MapExpert offers these capabilities plus additional customizing features.

MapExpert's annotation capability lets you highlight areas, outline routes or territories, and attach digital notes to maps. Once you have your map ready, you can preview and print black-and-white or color maps from within the program. MapExpert will even print out wall-sized maps.

Expert's *Travel Planner Gold*, available on CD-ROM or floppy disk, is the low-priced leader among the products here. Besides the requisite trip planning features, the CD version comes with extra bells and whistles, such as video clips and photographs of popular destinations. The videos are of the local tourist bureau variety, but they are informative. Expert's planner will also display time zones, list emergency numbers, and access airport and airline information. When you need help, the CD version of Travel Planner even talks to you; it will tell you more about where you'll be traveling and even suggest sights to visit.

Overall, Travel Planner is not as strong a program as the others, because the quality of its maps aren't up to standard. But for the price, it's a bargain.

## Trip Planning Software: Vendor Information

| Title | Price | Contact Information |
|---|---|---|
| Destination Europe | $50 (plus price of Road Atlas) | |
| Destination Ski | $30 (plus price of Road Atlas) | |
| Automap Streets | $40 | |
| AAA Trip Planner | $40 | Compton's New Media (800) 862-2206 |
| Map'n'Go | | DeLorme Mapping (207) 865-1234 |
| Street Atlas USA | $80 | |
| MapExpert | $295 | |
| Travel Planner Gold | $50 | Expert Software (800) 759-2562 |

**Travel Planner Gold: The low-priced leader**

Travel Planner Gold includes extra bells and whistles such as video and audio capability, but its maps aren't quite up to standard.

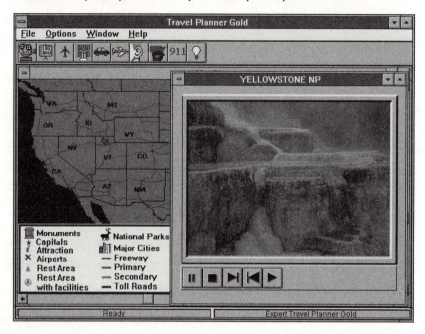

So next time you plan a trip, look to your computer. It can plan everything on your route so you won't have to roll down your car window and shout at strangers for directions. It's like having a built-in digital travel agent.

# Using a Spreadsheet to Track Car Repairs

Can you remember the last time you changed the oil in your car? Or how about the last time you rotated your tires—or even bought new tires? Although automotive records are important to properly maintain your car, they can be a nuisance to keep up. And while you can keep records the old-fashioned way—in a little notebook—using a computer spreadsheet database to track your car maintenance and repairs offers lots of advantages.

A database is simply a means to organize information and then derive summary data. For our car database, the information will be all of the maintenance and repairs we perform on our vehicle. The summary data will be information such as the date of the last oil change, the amount of money spent on oil changes in the past year, the amount of money spent for repairs over the past year or over the life of the vehicle, and so on.

## *Using a computer spreadsheet database to track your car maintenance and repairs offers lots of advantages.*

You can use any spreadsheet—Lotus 1-2-3, Microsoft Excel, or Quattro Pro, for example—to create your automotive tracking system. And you can view or sort your data any way you wish. For example, you can list transactions by date, by garage, by type of repair, or by cost. It's entirely up to you.

Here's how you can create your own automotive database. We'll use Lotus 1-2-3 Release 5 for our sample database. We'll create a basic structure within the spreadsheet that accepts automotive repair and maintenance data. This includes a description of the repair or maintenance itself, the service garage that did the work, the date the service was performed, the mileage on the car at the time of the service, and the cost. With this information, you can summarize your automotive expenses.

Within your spreadsheet, create the following columns along the top: Date, Repair/Maintenance, Type, Cost, Mileage, and Garage. Of course, you're free to add to or change these headings, but we'll keep them simple for this example. Here are our definitions:

| Date | The date the repair or maintenance was performed. Note that you will want to format this column to work in a date format: For more information on how to do this, consult your spreadsheet's documentation. In Lotus 1-2-3, highlight the column, then select Style, Numbers, and Date in the format you wish to use. If you don't use the date format, you won't be able to later search for transactions based on date—for example, you would be unable to track all repairs made during the last year. |

### Spreadsheet headings for the automobile tracking system

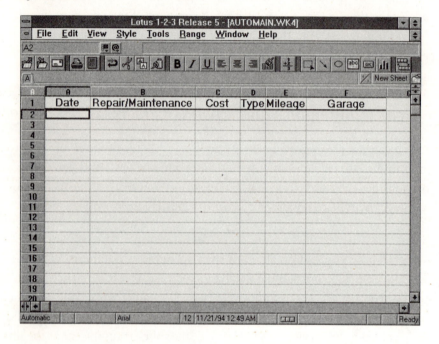

| Repair/ Maintenance | A description of repairs made to the car—oil change, distributor replacement, tune-up, and so on. |
|---|---|
| Type | Lets you designate R for repair and M for maintenance to easily distinguish repairs (replacing broken timing belts and fixing broken axles) from maintenance (oil changes and tune-ups). |
| Cost | Amount you paid for the repair or maintenance. You may want to format this column to work with money: For more information on how to do this in your particular spreadsheet, consult your user's guide. In 1-2-3, you highlight the column, select Style and Numbers, and then choose Currency with two digits. |
| Mileage | Your car's odometer reading at the time of the repair or maintenance. |

**TIP**

Don't forget to save your work along the way. In 1-2-3, access the File menu and choose Save As. Type in a name—for this example, let's use **AUTOMAIN**—and then select Save.

With your basic format in place, you're ready to enter repair and maintenance data. Each time you have work done to your car, enter the information into your spreadsheet. Let's add an entry for an oil change at Ziffy's Garage: As you can see, the process is straightforward.

→ **Adding the first entry to the auto maintenance spreadsheet**

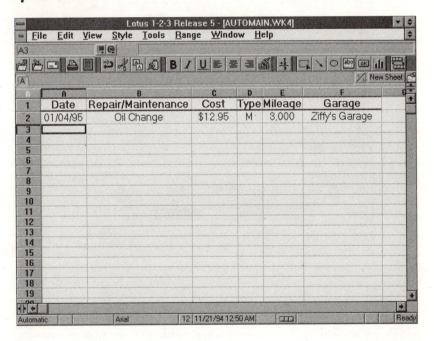

There are many ways to modify your spreadsheet to suit your needs. For example, you can choose to break down the repair/maintenance category. This may be useful if, for example, you have had an oil change and a flat tire fixed at the same time. Or, if you like, you can choose to treat labor rates as separate items. It's up to you.

**TIP**

The most important consideration is that you be consistent in your entries—otherwise, the computer won't be able to analyze the data correctly. For example, the computer can't tell that *oil change* and *oil changes* are the same item.

## Totaling the auto repair cost

Spreadsheet programs make it easy to determine the total cost of your automobile repairs.

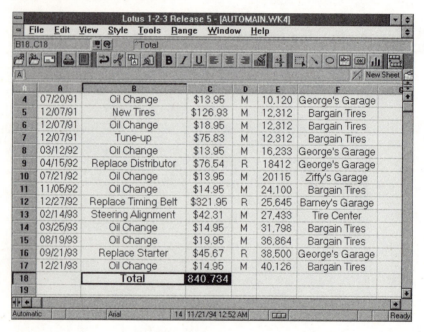

We've added data for a few years of maintenance and repairs on this sample vehicle. If you're using 1-2-3, select the spreadsheet cell immediately below the cost column and select the Sum tool: 1-2-3 automatically adds all the expenses for the column. If you're using another spreadsheet program, consult your user's guide on how to add column totals.

Let's find out how much money was spent for repairs in this example. (When you want to find out how much you've spent in other categories, the steps are identical; just call out the other fields.)

**1.** Highlight the entire spreadsheet table, including the headings. (Again, use the mouse to click on an extreme edge of the table and simply drag the mouse across all of the data.)

**2.** Access the New Query command under the Tools menu. (Note: Use the equivalent commands appropriate to your spreadsheet.)

**3.** Set the new table to begin at a different location by selecting the appropriate icon and setting it to start underneath the current table. This will prevent the new table from overlapping your existing one.

**4.** Select Set Criteria Menu. Under the Criteria menu, select Type as the field and select R as the value. Here, you're telling the program which records to look for—in this case, those with a type R for Repairs.

**5.** Select OK and look for the results.

**6.** To add totals, use the same method described above.

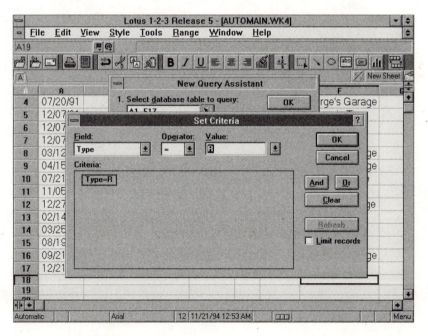

### Searching for all repairs with the Criteria menu

This basic automotive database will adequately organize your automotive records and give you a good idea of what your vehicle costs. When you want a hard copy, just print it out. Of course, this is just a start, and you are free to enhance the basic spreadsheet to better suit your needs as you become more accustomed to the concepts.

### ➡ After the search, the program lists the results

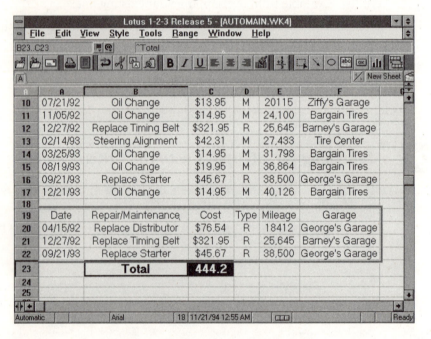

### ➡ Sorting: Organizing Your Data

As mentioned earlier, you can arrange your data in any order you wish through a process called sorting. Here's how to list your transactions by date, by garage (alphabetically), by mileage, or by any other field:

**1.** Highlight the entire data table by clicking on a spreadsheet cell at one end and dragging the cursor across all of the data.

### → Sorting: Organizing Your Data

**2.** In 1-2-3, access the Sort command by first selecting Range. Select the type of data (field) that you wish to use and how you want to order it in the column.

**3.** The spreadsheet will sort your data appropriately. (Note: By definition, we have already sorted the spreadsheet by date and mileage). For your spreadsheet, consult your documentation to see how to do this.

# "Are We There Yet?"

*"I'm hungry, Mom." "Johnny is reading my book." "I'm bored."*

If you're a parent, you've often heard these road "classics"—in fact, you probably said the same things yourself when you were a kid riding with your own parents. Of course, in those days we didn't have portable computers, television sets, or electronic game systems to entertain us. How times have changed! For road-weary parents, here are some portable computer activities that can help pass the time on those long drives.

One of the best ways to keep kids occupied with a portable computer on trips is to let them keep a journal to record their observations on the road. If you're venturing onto the vast unknown, you'll undoubtedly see wildlife, scenery, towns, and tourist traps, and you'll meet interesting people along the way. Your kids will experience new things, perhaps fishing or horseback riding, and they'll visit famous places and museums. All this can be recorded using a simple word processor on a portable computer. Best of all, when you return home, you can use each child's observations to create a booklet that will bring back trip memories for years to come.

Before the trip, install a word processor in your notebook computer and make sure that each child knows the basics of how to use it—at least how to open and save files and how to start and exit the application. Any word processor will do, but those included in application suites (which contain multiple applications) usually take up less hard-disk space than do the dedicated ones such as WordPerfect or Microsoft Word. Another choice might be a dedicated word processor/desktop publisher for kids, such as the Learning Company's Student Writing Center.

### Creating a road trip journal

You'll have a lifetime of memories and your kids will have hours of fun by making a journal of their observations on the road. All you need is a simple word processor and a portable computer.

Be sure that each child has a separate file. To help with file management, it's useful to create macros so each child only opens his or her own file. For example, ALT+A can open Amy's file, ALT+D is Dave's, and ALT+M is Matilda's. This way, there's less chance for one kid to accidentally alter another kid's file. (For more information on creating macros, consult your word processor's documentation.)

Of course, encourage your children to write down their ideas. For the younger ones, you can type in the comments they dictate to you.

*One of the best ways to keep kids occupied with a portable computer on trips is to let them keep a journal to record their observations on the road.*

When you get back home, use the layout features of your word processor to create a booklet. (All top-flight word processors have some basic desktop publishing capabilities.) A good way to organize the booklet is by events and places, in the order you saw them on the trip. For example, if stop one was a national park, you can insert excerpts from each child's comments on the park. You can also use separate sections for each child's individual viewpoint. Be sure to leave spaces in the text for pictures. After you've laid out the booklet and included space for the photos, you'll be ready to print your family album.

Of course, you can bring computer games to help pass the time on a long drive, though unfortunately, most games are geared for one player. Any computer magazine can make a number of good recommendations for games, and a visit to any software store will undoubtedly reveal a slew of games that kids will want to play.

**TIP**

A word of caution: When you choose a computer game, make sure that your portable computer can adequately run it. Most of the new flight simulators, for instance, have extensive system requirements. There's nothing more disappointing than firing up the computer on the road and finding that a game runs badly or not at all. Also, if you have monochrome graphics on your portable, make sure that the game is playable without color.

There are some games available that two or more people can play in the car. An excellent type of computer game for the road is the text adventure. You may remember Zork, HitchHiker's Guide to the Galaxy, and WishBringer, which were published by a company called Infocom. Although these programs are some ten years old, they still have play value, and sometimes you can find them on sale for a few dollars. Recently, Activision released the Zork Anthology, a series of these games on CD-ROM.

Text adventure games have no graphics or pictures, but offer puzzles within a rough storyline. In a car, a single player, the narrator, reads the dialog of the computer game while everyone else listens (this can be difficult if your car is noisy). Another person is in charge of "mapping," or drawing the layout of the world on paper as the character moves through it.

As you encounter puzzles, everyone contributes ideas on how to get through the locked doors or past the monsters. The beauty of these games is that they all play in your head and don't require graphics or sound. Note that easier text games like WishBringer may be best for traveling.

### Infocom Text Adventure Games

- ✔ HitchHiker's Guide to the Galaxy
- ✔ WishBringer
- ✔ Zork I
- ✔ Zork II
- ✔ Zork III
- ✔ Beyond Zork
- ✔ Zork Zero

Infocom is a division of Activision; you can obtain more information by calling (310) 479-5644 or (800) 477-3650.

Sports fans in the car can use the portable computer to play entire games of football or baseball—they can manage the team, call the plays, set the pitcher, and substitute players. We're not talking about full-graphic baseball and football games with arcade action, but text-based sports games. These include games from APBA, MicroLeague, and the Lance Haffner series of sports titles. As in a text adventure game, one person enters the commands and reads the results.

Each of the games features actual statistics of pro and college teams, and the computer determines the game's results by analyzing the statistics and each player's record. One person in the car can manage the 1927 New York Yankees, while the other person handles the seventies-era "Big Red Machine." In a way, it's like listening to sports on the radio. These games can be a blast to play, and they don't demand lots of memory the way graphic-based games do.

### Recommended Text-Based Sports Titles

✔ APBA Baseball (APBA)

✔ MicroLeague Baseball IV (MicroLeague)

✔ 3 in 1 College & Pro Football (Lance Haffner Games)

✔ Full Count Baseball (Lance Haffner Games)

✔ Final Four College Basketball (Lance Haffner Games)

For more information, contact Lance Haffner Games at (615) 242-2617, Micro-League at (302) 368-9990, or APBA at (800) 334-2722.

Other excellent games for travel are trivia or "edutainment" games that ask questions or give clues so players can solve a mystery. Some of the most popular of these games are Broderbund's *Where is Carmen San Diego* series, in which users play detective and analyze clues to track down the criminal Carmen wherever she may go.

In the Carmen geography games, the clues point to locations in the United States or the world, or even in outer space. In historical games, they refer to a time in history. During a car ride, families can play by having one person read the clues and the others contribute possible answers. Another player can also be the official researcher, looking up answers in the reference manuals that are included with all the Carmen San Diego games. There are similar games available from other publishers that use different characters.

### Recommended "Edutainment" Games

✔ Headline Harry (Davidson)

✔ Mario's Time Machine (Mindscape)

✔ Mario is Missing (Mindscape)

✔ Where in the World is Carmen San Diego? (Broderbund)

✔ Where in History is Carmen San Diego? (Broderbund)

✔ Where in Space is Carmen San Diego? (Broderbund)

✔ Where in Europe is Carmen San Diego? (Broderbund)

✔ Where in the USA is Carmen San Diego? (Broderbund)

For more information, contact Broderbund at (415) 382-7818, Davidson at (800) 545-7677, or Mindscape (415) 883-3000.

For a variation on a classic car game, you can play automotive bingo. Before the trip, use your computer to create bingo-style cards—but instead of the usual numbers, use symbols for things that the kids are likely to see on the road. Although you can use any draw or paint program to create such a game, the best choices are Windows Paintbrush or, even better, Broderbund's Kid Pix, with its collection of clip art.

### *Players call out any object they see along the road and cross out the corresponding picture on their cards.*

First, draw a grid using the program's line or box tools. Now, think of all the things that you could possibly see from the car: cars or trucks of certain colors (if you have a color printer), barns, bridges, birds, telephone poles, cows, horses, tunnels, signs, houses, buildings, and so on. Either draw icons or use clip art to represent each item, and randomly distribute them among the squares on your grid. Don't forget to mark the center square with an F for free.

The first step in creating auto bingo cards is to draw a simple grid.

Once the grid is filled, mark it with a small A in the top right corner and print a few copies. After that, you add new icons or rearrange existing ones, mark the rearranged grid with a B, print some more, and so on (the marks help prevent two players from getting the same card).

To play, distribute a crayon and a different bingo card to each player. Players call out any object they see along the road and cross out the corresponding picture on their cards. As in real bingo, the goal is to make a complete line across

➡ ## Setting up the travel bingo card

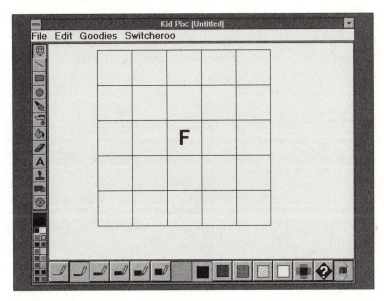

➡ ## Dressing up the bingo card

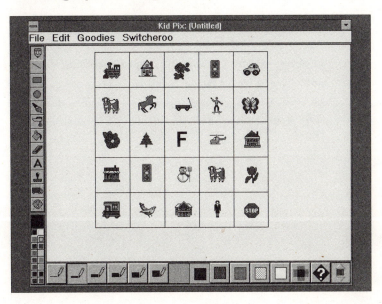

> ### ➜ *Make a destination-based crossword puzzle*
>
> Kids like crossword puzzles. When you're traveling, you can create one with words keyed to a place you're planning to visit. Several programs on the market let you create and print your own crossword puzzles, including Disney Software's Mickey's Crossword Puzzle Maker (1-800-688-1520) and a shareware program called Crossword Creator.
>
> During the trip, the kids will have fun recognizing the names of places they've visited; or, if you haven't gotten there yet, they'll learn more about their destination and they'll have fun recognizing the names when they do arrive.

the grid, either horizontally, vertically, or diagonally. The player who finishes a line first yells "Bingo!" and wins the game (while the others moan in unison).

When you're ready to take a trip, don't forget the computer. As we've seen, it can help organize your trip and then make traveling more enjoyable by providing entertainment along the way. And with your maintenance and repair logs, you'll be assured that your car is in shape to make the trek. Don't leave home without it. And Godspeed.

Wayne Kawamoto is a freelance writer in the computer industry, specializing in the areas of business, entertainment, and multimedia. He is a regular contributor to publications such as Computer Shopper magazine, Home Office Computer magazine, and many more. In his spare time, Wayne loves to travel with his three kids (and he's not afraid to ask for directions!).

# 4 | *Hotels and Resorts*

# Finding

safe, clean, and suitable lodging on your trip—never an easy task—can be made much easier through online flight reservations systems that you might already be using to book your air travel (see Chapter 2). In addition, many online services offer databases and other information related to hotels, inns, bed and breakfasts, and even cheap motels.

Here's an example: Not too long ago my wife and I decided to meet our son and his wife for a brief holiday in London before going on to Switzerland. We needed a hotel and had no clue how to book one ourselves. Experience had taught us that without some idea of what we wanted to pay and where we wanted to be, we were likely to be disappointed (if not ripped off).

Using our home computer, we were able to pick the location of the hotel, specify the maximum we wanted to pay, and even choose the type of bed we wanted. In a matter of minutes we searched an extensive database and came up with several that seemed to fit the bill. A few hours later we had confirmed reservations, confident that we had found lodgings we might otherwise have overlooked.

Admittedly, it may take some experimenting and a bit of dedication, and you may encounter a few blind alleys from time to time. But in the end it's worth the trouble—you'll save money as well as time.

## The ABCs of Online Hotel Booking

Before you start booking your travel through the variety of online services available, keep in mind that some of the databases we'll look at only provide information and phone numbers—actual reservations have to be made by telephone (this is true of the OAG hotel database, for instance—more on that later). But even if you do make the actual reservations online, always call the hotel to confirm.

Lodging services are available from many of the same reservations systems that make it possible to book airline tickets and rental cars, and we'll be examining several of these online services. They vary somewhat in the access they provide as well as the ease of use of their interfaces. Once you decide to begin booking your own travel, you'll find that most online providers offer some initial free access time to allow you to get a feel for the way their services and software work. When you find one you like, settle down with it, but don't make a full commitment until you do some experimenting.

If you talk with knowledgeable insiders in the travel industry, it won't be long before you run into a lot of odd names like *Sabre* (see Chapter 2), *Apollo*, *PARS*, and so on. These are *global distribution systems* (GDSs) to the travel industry, networks developed back in the 1960s that allow travel industry professionals to efficiently and easily book flights online. In the 1980s, GDSs grew to include rental cars, hotels, and more. When CompuServe, Prodigy, America Online, and other service providers came along, several consumer gateways to these GDS networks were offered. Eaasy Sabre and OAG are the most popular of the services, and they offer a variety of travel-related information.

Until now, only a small percentage of hotel reservations have been made through electronic booking. But all that is expected to change with the advent of more user-friendly products, the increasing popularity of the Internet, and the appearance of interactive cable TV. Big changes and new features are on the horizon if those in charge of the new online resources fulfill the promise of their advanced billing.

## How to Book a Hotel Using Eaasy Sabre

Though best known for its flight-reservation service, Eaasy Sabre also offers a worldwide hotel-booking service that is increasing in popularity. While this service is not the most comprehensive of its kind, Eaasy Sabre's hotel/motel reservation service offers you the advantage of making the actual reservation online, while other major services and databases only offer information.

You can get to the popular Eaasy Sabre service through many online services, such as Prodigy, CompuServe, Delphi, America Online, GEnie, and e-World. Using this program to book your lodging is quite easy. After logging on to Eaasy Sabre (see Chapter 2 for how to do this) simply choose Hotels from the Reservations menu. Remember that the following navigation commands are always available:

- ➡ /Help or ? for assistance
- ➡ /Res or /R to go to the Reservations Menu
- ➡ /Exit or /E to leave Eaasy Sabre

Once you're in the Hotel section, simply enter the city in which the hotel is required or the name of the airport in your destination city (*LAX* for the Los Angeles Airport, for example); your arrival and departure dates; and the number of adults in your room.

**NOTE** Don't worry about entering the three-letter code for your destination city. Simply type in the full name of the city and the corresponding code will pop up on the screen.

At this point, you can narrow down your options based on several factors:

- ➔ **Hotel name** If you know the name of the hotel, lets you proceed to its listing immediately.
- ➔ **Location** Allows you to specify location in a city, airport, resort, or suburb.
- ➔ **Transportation** Asks you whether or not you need transportation to the hotel.
- ➔ **Hotel chain** Allows you to specify a particular hotel chain.
- ➔ **Bed type** Allows you to specify number and/or type of bed.
- ➔ **Zip/postal code** Allows you to search in a specific zip or postal code.
- ➔ **Special room rate** Allows you to choose your hotel based on the corporate rates, senior rates, promotional rates, and other special rates it offers. (As they say in the trade, "Nobody pays the rack rate. That's the same as going into a car showroom and paying sticker price.")
- ➔ **Maximum room rate** Allows you to choose the maximum you want to pay for your room.
- ➔ **Area code** Allows you to search a specific area code.

Choosing the Hotels option produces a list of the hotels available that meet your criteria, along with their distance from the airport, room rate, and chain code. You can change the criteria at any time through Preferences until you actually choose your hotel.

### *Narrow down your lodging options*

Eaasy Sabre's Preferences box lets you choose a hotel based on a variety of criteria.

```
                    Hotel Preferences for
                      LOS ANGELES, CA
                Mon 06-Feb-1995 to Thu 09-Feb-1995

Transportation to Hotel (Y/N): N      Area Code of Hotel: ___
                                      Zip Code of Hotel:  _____

   Special Rates            Bed Type              Location
 [ ]No preference      No preference       No preference
 [ ]Corporate          One King            City
 [ ]Government         Two King            Suburban
 [ ]Military           One Queen           Airport
 [ ]Family Plan        Two Queen           Resort
 [ ]Senior Citizen     One Double
 [ ]Convention         Two Double
 [ ]Promotional        One Twin               [ OK ]    [ Cancel ]
 [ ]Weekend            Two Twin
```

At this point, we're ready to move on to the reservation process. Here's how that process works on Eaasy Sabre. You are given an abundance of information on the hotel you choose: the chain, hotel name, address, telephone, distance from airport, transportation available from airport, check-in time, required deposit/guarantee information, room rate, and your reservation dates. Once you've checked this information, you have the option of changing your preferences, changing your arrival or departure dates, viewing a description of the hotel, going back to the previous screen, reserving a room, or viewing other hotels.

If you choose to reserve a room, you are given the option of using your personal profile data, which may include specific credit information, room preferences, and much more, to complete your transaction. (Completing a personal profile will speed up the process considerably if you're a frequent traveler—see Chapter 2 for more information.) Or you may choose to provide another source of payment, such as another credit card or a check.

Next, Eaasy Sabre lets you enter special information (less than 72 characters) that you would like sent directly to the hotel, for example, **Request nonsmoking room above the third floor.** Once you've done this, you're all set. Eaasy

Sabre lets you review your reservation and gives you a confirmation number. Even after you've finished the reservation process, you're given the option of canceling at any time.

**NOTE** Don't forget to write down your confirmation number and take it with you on your trip. As any seasoned traveler knows, the reservation process is anything but foolproof, and many say that computer reservations systems leave even more room for error. If you have a confirmation number in hand, at least you'll have the satisfaction of blaming someone else for the error, and your reservation is more likely to be restored.

### Pros and Cons of Using Eaasy Sabre to Book Hotels

#### Pros

- Allows you to choose from thousands of hotels worldwide
- Lets you narrow down your options based on several criteria
- Makes it easy to reserve accomodations in larger cities
- Also gives you the option of making car rental arrangements for your destination

#### Cons

- Geared primarily to show hotels near airports. If the town where you want to stay is a smaller city, it may be tough finding a hotel. (Eaasy Sabre is reportedly in the process of remedying this problem.)

## How to Book a Hotel Using OAG

OAG (Official Airline Guide) was introduced many years ago as a voluminous, frequently updated printed compilation of airline schedules for travel agents, which allowed them to view all airline flights and connections in one place without having to piece together schedules from multiple airlines. Later OAG made an abridged version available to the public. The electronic version of OAG, available on CompuServe, GEnie, Dow Jones News/Retrieval, and the Internet, is used by the public and travel agents alike.

Like Eaasy Sabre, OAG is geared to airline travel. However, OAG, which includes over 50,000 hotel and motel listings in North America, Europe, and the Pacific, is more comprehensive than Eaasy Sabre. In addition to hotel and motel listings, OAG includes listings for bed and breakfasts, five-star resorts, and more—and every entry is rated by AAA. This greater and more diverse number of listings means you may have much better luck finding a hotel in a smaller town through OAG than through Eaasy Sabre.

> *In addition to hotel and motel listings, OAG includes listings for bed and breakfasts, five-star resorts, and more—and every entry is rated by AAA.*

**OAG lets you choose from a variety of lodging choices**

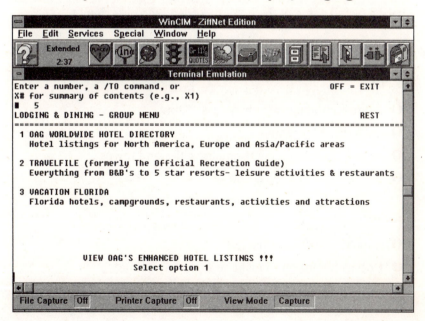

However, there are two significant disadvantages to OAG. First, unlike Eaasy Sabre, OAG imposes a substantial usage surcharge (see Chapter 2). Also, you can't actually make your reservation online though OAG, only find out what's available; you still have to book the reservation directly with the hotel or through your travel agent.

Using OAG is simple. Hotels and motels are listed in alphabetical order, along with the following information:

- Hotel/Motel Name
- Phone Number
- Address
- Price Range
- AAA Rating

For additional information on a specific hotel, you simply enter the line number of the entry. To proceed directly to a particular hotel or chain of hotels, enter the partial or full name of the hotel preceded by a plus sign (+).

## Pros and Cons of Using OAG to Book Hotels

### Pros

- More comprehensive than Eaasy Sabre
- Includes AAA ratings
- Easier to find lodging in smaller cities and towns
- Includes worldwide coverage

### Cons

- Imposes a hefty surcharge
- Doesn't allow you to make reservations online

# Other Information-Only Lodging Services

A variety of other lodging databases are available through the online services. CompuServe has the greatest selection of lodging databases. Here's some of what you'll find:

➜ **AA Accommodations**: A large database of accommodations available in Britain and Ireland, AA Accommodations—carried by CompuServe—is maintained by the UK's equivalent of AAA. This database includes a detailed collection of over 8,000 AA-inspected hotels, guest houses, inns, farmhouses, and campsites in Britain and Ireland. Each entry includes an AA rating along with a lengthy description, a listing of amenities, dates open, pricing, parking, type of credit cards accepted, and other useful information. As with OAG, you have to do the actual booking yourself. However, you have all the information you need to do so.

➜ **Lanier's Bed & Breakfast Database**: Based on the book *The Complete Guide to Bed and Breakfasts, Inns, and Guesthouses in the United States and Canada* by Pamela Lanier, this database in CompuServe contains detailed information on over 11,000 bed and breakfasts in the United States and Canada. Data includes location, phone and e-mail, amenities, types of meals served, bathrooms (private or shared), handicapped accessibility, accommodations for children and pets, price range, and more. Using the Bed & Breakfast Database is easy. You can search the database by b&b name or location. When searching by name, the system can search by a partial or full name. When searching by location, you can enter the specific city and state in which the bed and breakfast is located, you can search the whole state, or you can search by metropolitan area, which will return all of the bed and breakfasts in your chosen city and the surrounding metropolitan area. When you have narrowed your search, a listing of bed and breakfasts is provided. Note that this database does not provide information on the availability of rooms at any given time.

➜ **ABC Worldwide Hotel Guide**: This service, available as part of CompuServe's extended services (it costs more, but not as much as OAG), offers information on over 60,000 hotels worldwide. The depth of this information varies; some entries include little more than the basic description and pricing, and others include such eclectic data as the style of architecture or information on the region in which the hotel is located. Updated four times a year, the Worldwide Hotel Guide is similar to Eaasy Sabre in that it allows you to narrow your search by choosing from a list of criteria; and it is similar to OAG in its international focus and information-only format.

### Search for Unconventional Lodging by Unconventional Means

Many bed and breakfasts are "Mom and Pop" businesses, so they may use out of the ordinary—and inexpensive—ways to reach their prospective guests. Through CompuServe's Inn & Lodging Forum (GO BED) you might find tips on starting and operating a bed and breakfast, reviews of new places to visit, listings of haunted inns and other eclectic lodging, and much more from professionals in the field. Or try the classified section of your online service. If you're on CompuServe, check out the Government Give-aways forum, which provides information on, among other things, ways to travel cheaply. You never know what you might find.

### Figure 4.3

What you'll find in the Inn & Lodging Forum library

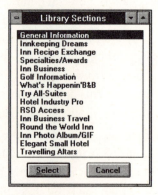

## *Find your perfect house in the country*

Lanier's Bed & Breakfast Database lets you search for your idyllic vacation spot by providing detailed descriptions of over 11,000 inns, guesthouses, and B&Bs around the United States and Canada. Whether you're looking for a tiny inn in Vermont or a spa in Calistoga, Lanier's will have the answers.

## Some Tips from the Experts

Many online aficionados find that the most serendipitous aspect of booking travel online is the people they meet. Though it may seem intimidating at first, you may find that posting your questions on travel forums will elicit many useful replies and handy tips from seasoned travelers.

In addition, many travelers post *postcards* on the CompuServe Travel Forum. Updated frequently, these postcards are candid, first-person reviews of hotels at nearly any given destination. Information provided on a postcard includes the location of the hotel, price, description, likes and dislikes about the lodging, and any other information (pertinent or not) the writer feels like including.

Here are some tips from seasoned online travel-planning veterans on making the best of online hotel booking:

From Heinz D. Trost: "My experience with hotel booking in Eaasy Sabre is that it's better to type in the code of the closest airport to the destination, so the chance is better of finding some hotels in unknown towns and villages."

From Rick Pike: "Eaasy Sabre tends to confirm reservations, then cancel them…don't ask why—I have no idea. What is particularly frustrating is to make a reservation, then confirm it by telephone, and *then*, after telephone confirming it, Eaasy Sabre cancels it. So, I use Eaasy Sabre as a resource tool, and make my reservations by telephone."

From Bonnie L. Kappler: "I have had some very good experiences using the (CompuServe) classifieds. It is quite inexpensive to advertise 'for' info, but I have been able to find many really great things already listed. I went to London to the theater last year and was able to rent a three-bedroom flat (with butler ) for less than $100 total per night. It was wonderful, with great location and transportation. If you are not using a "name" hotel, however, I would guess that there is a risk. The one I found mailed me good pictures and a local map that gave me enough information to find my way around."

From Ron Rodrigues: "Make sure you retain both the Sabre confirmation number as well as the confirmation number generated by the hotel chain. With both of these numbers, I've never had a problem after making hundreds of Eaasy Sabre airline, hotel, and car reservations."

From G.C. Bellaire: "I use Eaasy Sabre from time to time to book hotels. It is okay, but not great. The biggest problem is that it doesn't always give you the lowest rate. For example, if there is a special going on, the rate may not appear in Eaasy Sabre—nor do specially negotiated rates, over and above "standard" corporate rates.... For little towns, you may do well to query hotels for the nearest reasonably sized airport and then just scroll through your listings. The more pages you scroll, the more distant from the airport the listings become (as a rule). Eventually you may hit listings in the small town you're interested in. Or, if the town you are interested in has an airport with commercial service, so much the better. Just use that city's airport code."

There's a big world of information out there waiting to be tapped. Though sometimes it may simply be more efficient to plug in to your friendly travel agent or call the 800 numbers for hotel chains to make your reservation, chances are you'll enjoy discovering for yourself those neat places you'd otherwise miss, both at home and abroad.

Jack E. Buttram is an air transport-rated pilot, broadcaster, writer, photographer, ham radio operator, steam engine buff, and near computer geek; but he makes his living as a public affairs consultant with offices in Washington, DC and Greenville, SC. He has served as a staffer in the U.S. Senate and the White House. He and his wife, Barbara, have five children and 13 grandchildren.

# 5 *International Formalities*

# International

travel planning in today's high-tech world means that any traveler with a computer and modem can research and book a flight to Frankfurt, locate a hotel in Hong Kong, see what the State Department has to say about travel in Togo, and talk with locals in Luxembourg about the best restaurants and sights, all from the comfort of home.

International travelers have special needs that people traveling within the United States don't have. They need to get a passport and possibly a visa, find out about safety and the political situation in their target destination, and often learn to cope with another language. This chapter will cover the resources available for your computer that will make an international trip easier and more enjoyable.

## Finding State Department Information Online

The State Department issues consular information sheets for American travelers going abroad, covering topics such as entry requirements, facilities, crime, adoptions, dual nationality, drug penalties, civil aviation oversights, and embassy location and registration. The State Department also provides three levels of advisory. A *warning* recommends deferral on all travel to a particular country. A *caution* indicates that there may be unstable conditions or health problems. A *notice* advises travelers of inconveniences, currency changes, and crime conditions.

### Places to Access the State Department Advisories

- ✔ CompuServe (GO STATE)
- ✔ America Online (keyword TRAVEL)
- ✔ OAG (in the Worldwide Travel Facts menu)
- ✔ The State Department BBS (202-647-9225)
- ✔ Internet Gopher (St. Olaf College, Internet Resources, US-State-Department-Travel-Advisories)
- ✔ Internet e-mail subscription (send e-mail to travel-advisories-request@stolaf.edu and ask to subscribe to the travel advisories list)

## *Consular information sheet on CompuServe*

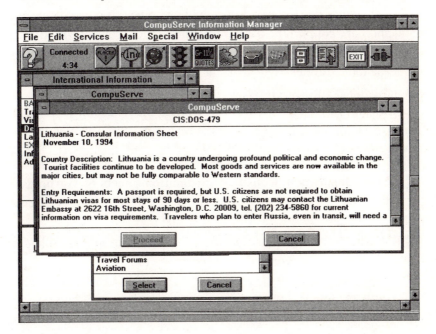

# Finding Passport and Visa Information Online

Several major online services provide information about current passport and visa regulations. These services are all good choices if you just want to find out a particular country's passport and visa requirements. If you want a service to handle all your visa needs, however, check out Visa Advisors (GO VISA) on CompuServe. Visa Advisors lists visa and passport requirements for over 200 countries and offers a passport and visa expediting service (for a fee).

## Places to Access Passport and Visa Information

- ✔ CompuServe (GO VISA)
- ✔ OAG (in the Worldwide Travel Facts World Travel Guide)
- ✔ Prodigy (JUMP TRAVEL)

## Resources on Multiple Online Services

Previous chapters have discussed in detail how to use an online flight reservation system and have covered the basic travel information available on the major on-line services; each of these services also provides specific features of interest to the international traveler. Here are some suggestions on where to look for the most detailed international travel information.

Of the three main flight information services (Eaasy Sabre, Worldspan, and OAG), *OAG (Official Airlines Guide)* provides the most information for the international traveler. OAG's Worldwide Travel Facts menu includes the following:

- **State Department Consular Information Sheets & Warnings** offers the State Department advisories discussed in "Finding State Department Information Online," earlier in this chapter.

- **World Travel Guide** includes detailed information on hundreds of countries around the world. This guide covers the following topics: population, geography, language, time, passport and visa requirements, money, duty free, public holidays, health, travel, accommodations, resorts, excursions, leisure, business and social customs, the economy, history, government, and climate.

- **Currency Exchange Rates** lists exchange rates for all major international currencies.

- **Accu-Weather Forecasts** provides detailed weather forecasts for 450 major cities. Forecasts are updated hourly.

- **World of Information** offers encyclopedic information on hundreds of countries around the world. This comprehensive database includes information on hotels, useful addresses, local information sources, banking, business procedures, health precautions, currency, transportation, holidays, social customs, politics, and history. World of Information is similar to the World Travel Guide, but contains more business information.

OAG's Lodging and Dining Menu includes the OAG Worldwide Hotel Directory, which has international listings primarily in Europe, Asia, and the Pacific. In addition to its online format, OAG's flight information is available on disk through its product FlightDisk, which recently introduced a worldwide edition.

## Places to Find OAG

✔ CompuServe (GO OAG)

✔ GEnie (keyword: OAG)

✔ Dow Jones News/Retrieval

✔ The Internet (send e-mail to info@aog.com for details)

*Fodor's Worldview*, a "just-in-time" travel information service, provides current travel information in conjunction with Fodor's Travel Publications. Each month you can preview a new location online with details on business services (computer rentals, mail, messengers, translations, photocopying, and so on), cuisine, nightlife, entertainment, music, tours, special events, shopping, fitness, spectator sports, museums, and transportation. The main advantage of this feature is that it offers up-to-the minute travel information as well as basic travel details about a location. You can also order Worldview Profiles for other locations online for a small fee.

## ➡ Fodor's Worldview on Prodigy

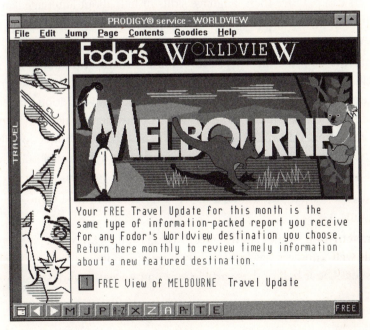

### Places to Find Worldview

✔ Prodigy (JUMP WORLDVIEW)

✔ eWorld (shortcut: FODORS)

✔ the Internet—via the Global Network Navigator (GNN) Travelers' Center (send e-mail to info@gnn.com for more details)

# Resources on Specific Online Services

Each of the major online services carries unique travel resources in addition to the ones available on multiple services. For example, along with the State Department travel advisories, America Online also offers several unique features on international travel:

➡ **International House** (keyword: IES) regularly holds foreign language chats in French, Spanish, German, Portuguese, Russian, and other languages. It also includes a message board called the Cosmopolitan, where users can practice their language skills or talk about language learning. This is a good area to explore if you speak or are learning the language of your intended destination.

➡ **Internet Connection** (keyword: Internet) offers a number of international travel resources, including the Green Travel Mailing List (on ecotourism), Health Information for International Travel, Moon Travel Handbooks information, and US State Department Travel Advisories, in the Gopher and WAIS Databases area. The Internet Connection also offers access to newsgroups such as rec.travel.europe and rec.travel.asia.

➡ **Travel Forum** (keyword: Travel) includes the World Traveler Board, with more than 12,000 postings on international travel from America Online users.

➡ **Travel Holiday** (keyword: Travel Holiday) offers an online version of this well-known magazine, with excerpts from its current and back issues. About half of these articles are on international destinations.

➡ **Travelers' Corner** (keyword: Travelers Corner) includes International Profiles, which offers basic profiles on dozens of countries from Afghanistan to Zimbabwe. Each profile includes an introduction, snapshot, what to do there, do's and don'ts, and "potpourri." The Exotic Destinations Message Center contains thousands of user postings on exotic travel, with an emphasis on Europe, Asia, and Africa.

➡ ### Travelers' Corner on America Online

Find out about exotic destinations or places closer to home with this America Online service.

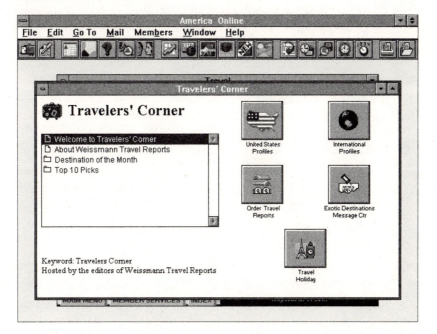

➡ **Weather** (keyword: Weather) covers weather in most large international cities.

➡ **Winery Travel Guide** (keyword: Travel) includes descriptions of wine-related travel in France, Germany, and Italy.

Prodigy offers several exclusive resources for the international traveler:

- **Travel Bulletin Board** (JUMP TRAVEL BB) contains hundreds of user messages on topics including Asia, Europe, Latin America, and international travel in general.

- **Travel Sources** (JUMP TRAVEL) offers the following topics: Foreign Exchange Rates, How to Get a Passport, and Travel Advisory Info; also includes details on where to find information about health and safety around the world.

- **Weather** (JUMP INTERNAT'L WEATHER) includes an International Weather section with weather information on cities around the world.

CompuServe's international travel resources are extensive, in part because of its numerous overseas users. These resources include the following:

- **ABC Worldwide Hotel Guide** (GO ABC) offers a searchable database of more than 60,000 hotels in over 200 countries around the world. Each entry includes an address, location information, telephone number, listing of facilities and business services, and credit card information. Some entries include more detailed descriptive information about the hotel and its surroundings.

- **Adventures in Travel** (GO AIT) provides a library of travel articles. Some recent articles include "Dutch Cheese Country," "Germany's Romantic Road," "Hong Kong's Vitality," and "Australia's Melbourne."

- **Foreign Language Forum** (GO FLEFO) offers excellent resources for anyone interested in learning or practicing a language before an overseas trip. The forum includes sections on the Spanish/Portuguese, French, German, Eastern European, Asian, and Italian languages as well as one on computers and languages. The library contains many interesting foreign language shareware programs.

➡ **Information USA/International** (GO LESKO) includes 36 files on international travel topics. Select Vacations and Business Travel (#12) from the initial menu, then International Travel (#4) from the submenu to view these documents. Topics range from passports to customs, travel safety, and even Arctic polar expeditions.

➡ **Inn & Lodging Forum** (GO INNFORUM) contains many files on international bed-and-breakfast inns in the library.

➡ **Internet Forum** (GO INETFORUM) contains a useful zipped library file, TRAVEL.ZIP, that provides information on travel resources on the Internet, including many references to international travel.

➡ **Travel Forum** (GO TRAVSIG) has numerous files, graphics, and messages of interest to the global traveler. Specific sections include Australia-New Zealand-South Pacific, Western Europe, Eastern Europe, Mexico/Central America, South America, and Africa/Middle East.

➡ **UK Accommodation & Travel Services** (GO UKTRAVEL) includes comprehensive information about travel in the UK and is divided into several subcategories:

   ➡ **AA Accommodation** (GO UKACCOMM) offers a database of more than 8,000 hotels, guest houses, inns, farmhouses, and campsites in Britain and Ireland. Each entry is rated by the UK's Automobile Association (AA) and includes a detailed description.

   ➡ **AA Restaurants** (GO UKREST) offers a searchable database of AA-recommended restaurants, including address, telephone number, rating, and a detailed description listing cuisine type, credit cards accepted, and average prices.

   ➡ **AA Golf Courses** (GO UKGOLF) provides information on more than 2,000 golf courses in the UK and Ireland, including details on location, phone number, course description, green fees, and other club information.

   ➡ **AA Days Out** (GO UKDAYSOUT) lists more than 2,000 things to do in the UK, including ideas for spending a day out at a castle, park, museum, art gallery, zoo, garden, or historical building. Each listing includes location, phone number, description, as well as details on opening times, entrance fees, and more.

➲ **Travel Britain Online** (GO TBAONLINE) includes news on travel in Britain and an e-mail connection to the British Tourist Authority as well as access to two searchable databases, Travel Britain Online and London Online. Travel Britain Online contains more than 1,000 entries on entertainment events, fairs, concerts, sporting events, exhibitions, and plays throughout Britain. London Online includes similar information, as well as a listing of places to have afternoon tea and recommended pubs. Each entry provides a detailed description, including location, dates, times, and prices.

Many of CompuServe's geographic-specific forums offer travel-related articles and photos in their libraries. These forums are a good way to get answers to your travel questions, often from locals of that country.

## Suggested Geographic-Specific Forums on CompuServe

✔ CompuServe Pacific Forum (GO PACFORUM)
✔ Japan Forum (GO JAPAN)
✔ Netherlands Forum (GO NETHERLANDS)
✔ Hong Kong Forum (GO HONGKONG)
✔ European Forum (GO EUROPEAN)
✔ UK Forum (GO UK)

In addition to access to OAG, GEnie offers many other features for the international traveler:

➲ **Deutschland RoundTable** (keyword: GERMANY) provides a link between American and German users. The RoundTable includes many files about travel and life in German-speaking countries and offers RTCs (Real Time Conferences) in German and English. Formerly the Germany and Europe RoundTable, this section has recently sprouted two new RoundTables—the British Isles RoundTable (keyword: BRITISH) and the Europe RoundTable (keyword: EUROPE).

- **Japan RoundTable** (keyword: JAPAN) offers a way for users from both the United States and Japan to communicate about everything Japanese—language, culture, music, food, business, and travel. The RoundTable offers frequent RTCs with both Japanese and English speakers.
- **Travel RoundTable** (keyword: TRAVEL) includes numerous files relating to international travel in its library, as well as an active bulletin board for messages.

## Online Services: Contact Information

| Online Service/Provider | Toll-free Number for Information |
|---|---|
| America Online | (800) 827-6364 |
| CompuServe | (800) 848-8990 |
| eWorld | (800) 775-4556 |
| GEnie | (800) 638-9636 |
| OAG | (800) 323-4000 |
| Prodigy | (800) PRODIGY |
| Worldview | (800) 799-9609 |

# Independent Travel BBSs

Several small, independent BBSs (bulletin board systems) devoted to travel also exist. Here are some of the best:

- **Europe Through the Back Door** offers book updates, travel tips, and recommendations for fans of Rick Steve's *Europe Through the Back Door* travel guide series.
- **Mexico Online** provides detailed information on Mexico, including news, travel tips, magazine articles, and book excerpts, sponsored by the Mexican government's tourism office, Moon Travel Handbooks, and the Mexican consulate.

➡ **The Travel Connection** covers a wide range of travel topics, with extensive international coverage. Includes travel tips, classifieds, bargain alerts, graphic files, travel-related shareware, online brochures, and State Department information. This is a subscription-based BBS.

## Travel-Related BBSs: Numbers to Dial

| Bulletin Board System (BBS) | Dial Via Modem: |
|---|---|
| Europe Through the Back Door | (206) 771-1902 |
| Mexico Online | (407) 582-7801 |
| The Travel Connection | (415) 691-0954 |

## Best Bets for the International Traveler

| If you're looking for... | Try |
|---|---|
| A bulletin board to leave messages on international travel | CompuServe's Travel Forum (or one of its many geographic-specific forums) |
| Detailed country information | OAG's World Travel Guide or World of Information |
| Foreign language information/practice | CompuServe's Foreign Language Forum or America Online's International House |
| Hotel information | CompuServe's ABC Worldwide Hotel Guide or OAG's Worldwide Hotel Directory |
| Travel safety information | State Department Travel Advisories |
| Up-to-the-minute travel information | Fodor's Worldview |
| Overall international travel information | CompuServe |

### ➡ Where to Get Answers to Your International Travel Questions

**TIP**

If you're looking for international travel information that you haven't been able to find from other sources (either printed or electronic), try leaving a message on an online service's international travel bulletin board. This is often the best way to ferret out the latest on happenings in foreign places—what not to miss, what to avoid, where those hidden gems are that other travelers don't know about. One caveat: Remember that the users who reply to you may not necessarily have the same taste as you do. What one person says is wonderful, inexpensive, and so on may not meet your definition of the word.

## CD-ROMs for the International Traveler: The Next Best Thing to Being There

Today's multimedia technology makes virtual visits to countries around the world and historical eras long past a reality. After ensuring that you have the proper hardware and software to run a multimedia CD-ROM, try some of the following titles:

- ➡ **Asia Alive** tours the countries of Asia and the Pacific—Cambodia, China, Vietnam, Hong Kong, Laos, Singapore, Malaysia, Indonesia, Australia, New Zealand, South Korea, Japan, Taiwan, and the Philippines—and includes detailed information on 20 major cities. It uses maps, video clips, music, and slides to make Asia come alive, while also providing tips and cultural information for the traveler.

- ➡ **Europe Alive** explores 15 European countries, using a combination of video, music, photos, maps, and text. In addition to featuring the countries of western Europe, *Europe Alive* also includes five activities for children ages 7 and up: Euro-Timeline, which explores 4,000 years in the history of Europe; Name That Flag and Anthem; Dizzy Aunt Lulu's Photo Album, which allows you to identify famous European landmarks; What

### *What You Need to Run a Multimedia CD-ROM*

| System | Minimum Requirements |
|---|---|
| Windows PC | 386SX microprocessor |
| | MPC compatible CD-ROM drive |
| | 4 MB RAM |
| | Super VGA monitor with 256 colors |
| | Microsoft Windows 3.1 with Multimedia Extensions |
| | DOS 3.1 or later |
| | Sound card and speakers |
| | Microphone (to record) |
| Macintosh | Color Macintosh |
| | CD-ROM drive |
| | 2MB RAM in System 6.0x or 4MB RAM in System 7 |
| | Microphone (to record) |

Country Can It Be?; and Country Capital Quest!. With this program, adults and children can explore Europe individually or as a family.

➜ **Exploring Ancient Architecture** offers travelers to England, France, Egypt, Greece, or Italy an opportunity to explore the history and architecture of the places they are about to visit. *Exploring Ancient Architecture* visits Stonehenge, the Dolman Tomb, the Temple of Khons, the Mortuary Temple of Mentuhotep, the Parthenon, the Ecclesiasterion, and Rome's Basilica of Constantine. The program uses three-dimensional animation, combined with historical narration, to make these architectural masterpieces come alive.

➜ **TVNZ New Zealand Encyclopedia** offers an outstanding introduction to New Zealand, its culture, and its natural beauty. Searchable by location or category, the program includes 1,200 photos, 70 videos, and 20 maps, and it covers 1,800 topics. This encyclopedia is comprehensive, covering everything from agriculture to sports, ecology, government, the arts, people, health, animals, and history. Video topics include Maori culture, sheep farming, yachting, and Rotorua.

### A wealth of information at your fingertips

Through maps, video, music, and text, today's multimedia CD-ROMs can help you explore the culture and history of your international destination before you arrive, and then help you find your way around when you get there.

● **New Zealand Birds** is an excellent companion to *TVNZ New Zealand Encyclopedia* for nature lovers and photography buffs. It includes over 500 images and detailed descriptions of the native birds of New Zealand, all searchable by bird name. The CD offers many tips on bird photography as well as a section called "Glimpses of New Zealand," with video clips of bungee jumping, the Bay of Islands, Mount Cook, and more.

● **World Beat** is an innovative program that explores the world's music and its impact on culture, *World Beat* includes video and music clips covering over 165 musical styles in more than 80 countries. By selecting a part of the world from the revolving globe, you can explore a musical style from that area. Or, you can choose a style from the style list—anything from andean to garfuno to zydeco. The program also includes interactive documentaries on African, Asian, and Latin American music; articles on world music; a list of nearly 20,000 albums and artists; and a music studio that lets you experiment with different musical styles.

**World Beat: Explore music around the world**

## Before You Go: Learning the Language on Your Computer

One obstacle that many international travelers need to overcome is the language barrier. In addition to the traditional language-learning methods—classroom instruction and audio-tape courses—you can also use your computer as a language-learning tool. Numerous foreign language software and CD-ROM titles have been introduced in the past few years, giving the computer-literate language learner a wide variety of choices.

## CD-ROM Travel Titles: Vendor Information

| Title | Price | Contact |
|---|---|---|
| Asia Alive<br>Europe Alive | $49<br>$49 | MediAlive<br>(408) 752-8500 |
| Exploring Ancient Architecture<br>World Beat | $60<br>$60 | Medio Multimedia<br>(800) 788-3866 |
| New Zealand Birds<br>TVNZ New Zealand Encyclopedia | $99 (NZ)<br>$99 (NZ) | Teamwork Multimedia Limited<br>++ 64 4 293 2137 (fax)<br>francis_g@kosmos.wcc.govt.nz<br>(Internet) |

Here are some suggested language programs:

● **Berlitz Live!** (Sierra)   This CD-ROM series offers an entertaining and informative way to learn a new language that takes full advantage of multimedia technology. The program is divided into several topics, including language essentials, hotels, business, using the phone for business, and eating out. The program is guided by an interactive animated tutor and combines games and cultural notes with language and vocabulary development. Available in Japanese and Spanish.

● **Berlitz Think 'n' Talk** (HyperGlot)   This series uses the "Berlitz Method" of instruction, with limited English intervention. Each of the 50 lessons in this comprehensive program uses animation and sound and includes four learning sections (Listen & Understand, Read, Write, and Think & Talk) and several exercises to reinforce what you've learned. A solid basic program, offered in Spanish, French, German, and Italian.

● **Learn to Speak 4.0** (HyperGlot)   This CD-ROM series takes the components of a traditional foreign language course and updates it with nineties technology. Each chapter focuses on a specific situation (arriving in the country or at the hotel, making an appointment) and contains a movie, vocabulary drills, and practical exercises, as well as listening and communication tests. The series also includes cultural notes and an online grammar reference and is suitable for both beginning and intermediate learners. Available in French and Spanish.

➡ **Berlitz Live!: Learn a language the multimedia way**

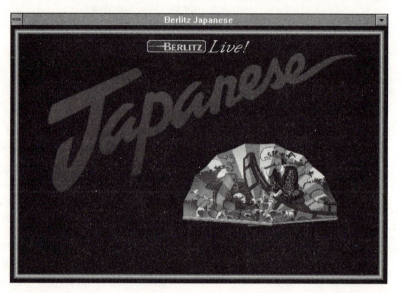

➡ **Lyric Language** (Penton Overseas)  If you're planning on traveling with your children, this CD-ROM is an excellent choice. *Lyric Language*, available in either French or Spanish, introduces your child to a foreign language through video, songs, and games. Adults can learn something as well. Your children will recognize the Family Circus comic strip kids in this series.

If you want to improve basic skills, or supplement one of the above courses with some additional training in a specific area, consider these options:

➡ **Languages of the World** (NTC Publishing)  This CD-ROM is a comprehensive multilingual dictionary with more than 7 million words in 12 languages. *Languages of the World* is compiled from well-known dictionaries, including both basic language dictionaries and business, science, and technical dictionaries. Languages include Chinese, Danish, Dutch, English, Finnish, French, German, Italian, Japanese, Norwegian, Spanish, and Swedish. This program is an outstanding reference for the language learner and is a great companion to the other programs in this list.

→ **PictureIt!** (Penton Overseas)   This software program is a suitable vocabulary development tool for the whole family. You can use it to learn new vocabulary or to create flashcards or multiple-choice tutorials to reinforce words already learned. The program contains more than 500 pictures, each of which includes the option to hear its pronunciation; some pictures incorporate animation and sound. Available in Spanish, French, German, and Italian.

→ **The Rosetta Stone** (Fairfield Language Technologies)   A good companion for people wanting practice in listening and writing skills, this program is based on a variety of multiple-choice tutorials that require the user to match a written or spoken word or phrase to a photograph. *The Rosetta Stone* also allows users to record their own voices to compare pronunciation. Available in Spanish, French, German, or Russian.

→ **Video Linguist** (Cubic Media)   This CD-ROM is a good choice for people who already have a basic knowledge of the language, but who want to improve their listening skills before an overseas trip. The program consists of 39 lessons covering such topics as the arts, travel, sports, and food, and is based on video clips from the target country's news media. It includes an electronic dictionary for vocabulary assistance and is suitable for intermediate to advanced learners, although beginners could also improve their comprehension skills with this program. Available in French or Spanish.

→ **VocabuLearn** (Penton Overseas)   One of the most comprehensive vocabulary development tools available, this is an excellent companion  for those wishing to develop their command of a language. *VocabuLearn* is available as a software program (Macintosh, DOS, and Windows) in Spanish, French, Italian, German, Japanese, Russian, or Hebrew and on CD-ROM in French or Spanish. Includes two audio cassettes.

Practice and immersion into the sound and "feel" of the language you are studying are the keys to success in language learning, and also the keys to opening once-closed doors to you abroad. The smallest amount of advance preparation can enhance any attempt at human communication—and can add enrichment to any overseas trip.

## Language Programs: Further Information

| Title | Price | Recommended for | Contact Information |
|---|---|---|---|
| Berlitz Live! | $99 Windows, Macintosh | Beginning through intermediate; Adults | Sierra (800) 743-7725 |
| Berlitz Think & Talk | $199 Windows, Macintosh | Beginning; Adults | HyperGlot (800) 800-8270 |
| Language of the World | $130 DOS $150 Windows, Macintosh | Beginning through advanced; Adults | NTC Publishing (800) 323-4900 |
| Learn to Speak Series v4.0 | $179 Windows, Macintosh | Beginning through intermediate; Adults | HyperGlot (800) 800-8270 |
| Lyric Language | $50 Windows, Macintosh | Beginning through intermediate; Children | Penton Overseas (800) 748-5804 |
| PictureIt! | $70 DOS, Windows, Macintosh | Beginning through intermediate; Adults and children | Penton Overseas (800) 748-5804 |
| The Rosetta Stone | $395 (complete series) $99 (first 22 lessons in four languages) | Beginning through intermediate; Adults and children | Fairfield Language Technologies (800) 788-0822 |
| Video Linguist | $100 Windows, Macintosh | Intermediate through advanced; Adults | Cubic Media (800) 232-8242 |
| VocabuLearn | $60 Macintosh $70 Windows | Beginning through advanced; Adults and children | Penton Overseas (800) 748-5804 |

## ➜ *Tips for Learning a Foreign Language*

**TIP**

✔ Review your material frequently. Language researchers have determined that a word or phrase must be repeated up to 45 times before it is retained; therefore, constant repetition of what you've learned is crucial. If remembering vocabulary is troublesome, get some index cards and make flash cards to test yourself on difficult words or purchase a vocabulary development program.

✔ Speak the language. Talk with native speakers to help your listening comprehension skills and develop your vocabulary. When you're alone, practice expressing yourself without concern for linguistic perfection. This will enhance your ability to speak and you can perfect your grammar and vocabulary as you continue to learn your new language.

✔ Use all your senses to immerse yourself in the language and its culture. Watch foreign films and TV shows, listen to the music of your target country, and taste its native foods. In large metropolitan areas you may also be able to experience this culture by visiting its ethnic neighborhood in your city.

*Patrice-Anne Rutledge* is a freelance writer specializing in technology, business, and travel. Patrice writes a monthly column on international business, *Global Business Today*, and is the co-author of three computer books. She began her career as a translator/interpreter, speaks six languages, and frequently uses computer resources to plan her many travels.

# 6 *Tips for Bargain Hunters*

**You** don't have to be well endowed financially to book travel on your computer. Whether you're a student on a budget, a world traveler with a limited bank account, or just someone who doesn't mind roughing it to get the best prices, there are resources at your disposal. You just might have to search a little more to find them.

## The Internet: The Highway of Choice for the Student Traveler

While many people prefer the friendliness and ease of use of the commercial on-line services to the at times incomprehensible and baffling Internet, the latter choice is the more logical one for most students. After all, an Internet account may be the only thing university students get for free. Fortunately, finding information through the Internet is a lot easier than it used to be, thanks to the World Wide Web. The World Wide Web (also referred to as WWW or the Web) is a way of accessing information on the Net that utilizes hypertext links, allowing pages of different files on the Internet to be connected and accessed easily. In the past few years, the Web's growth has been phenomenal. At the moment, none of the online services offer Web access, but as the Web grows, the services are scrambling to put together gateways (America Online is promising a gateway by winter 1995). Adding to the Web's ease of use are browsers such as Mosaic and Lynx, both available for free on the Net. These browsers have graphical interfaces that make the Web even easier to navigate.

> *An Internet account may be the only thing university students get for free.*

Finding travel information on the Internet is a lot easier these days thanks to the Global Network Navigator Travelers' Center, a free Internet travel publication available on the Web. The Global Network Navigator (GNN) is a service that organizes access to information on the Internet, using a full-color, easy to use, point-and-click graphical interface. In addition to the Travelers' Center, GNN offers similar services for music, education, and computers. The Travelers' Center contains graphical links to over 400 Internet travel resources. This multiplatform Web page uses hypertext links to essentially map out the Internet for travelers, allowing users to jump from one page to another with relative ease.

> ### The Travelers' Center contains graphical links to over 400 Internet travel resources.

The Travelers' Center is divided into three parts:

- ➡ *Notes from the Road*, a weekly magazine. This section includes regular columns from popular travel writers—a recent example is a weekly column by popular travel writer Jeff Greenwald on his bicycle trip around the world.
- ➡ *Internet Resources*, the travelers map of the Internet. At the click of a button, you can view map archives, youth hostel guides for the United States and Canada, uploads from a bicycle trip through Vietnam, interactive language programs and dictionaries, train schedules, and much more.
- ➡ *The Marketplace*, a "cybermall" in which travel companies can post information about their products and services.

The best thing about the Travelers' Center, and about the Internet in general, is that it's free. All you need is Mosaic, Lynx, or another graphical browser and access to the World Wide Web. If you have the appropriate browser and Web access, you can register for Travelers' Center via the Web at http://nearnet.gnn.com/ or via e-mail at form@gnn.com. To find out more about what you need to view GNN (such as Mosaic or Lynx) and how to get it, send a request via e-mail to access@gnn.com.

Some of the more hip travel guidebooks are also slowly making their foray into the Web scene. Lonely Planet recently introduced its Web page at http:\\www.digital.com\gnn\bus\lp\index.html, which includes a monthly newsletter and a list of its titles. Soon to be added are country profiles for every area covered by the Lonely Planet, a list of booksellers that carry its products, and more. (This information can also be accessed via e-mail at lonely@crl.com.) Other travel guides have similar Web pages in the works.

~🖥~

Gopher, which is a useful tool for finding specific resources on the Internet, may also be helpful in finding travel information. *Gopher* is menu-driven client/server software designed to organize certain Internet information; gopher *servers* are sites that provide menus of Internet resources, organized in various ways; these servers are accessed with gopher *client* software. Some of these sites are accessible through America Online, but even with the improved interface AOL uses, the information on gopher servers is a bit unstable.

A few gopher sites worthy of note for the traveler are the University of Manitoba and the Moon Travel Handbook. The University of Manitoba has an extensive menu of travel information. The Moon Travel Handbook gopher includes catalogs of Moon Travel's books, a newsletter, and information on how to order their books online. Moon Travel is also available via e-mail at travel@moon.com, and via the Web at http://www.moon.com:7000/.

➡ **Gopher Travel information on America Online**

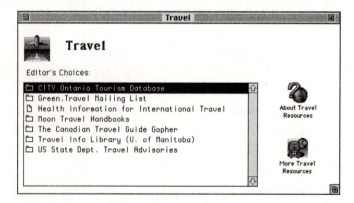

~🖥~

Several travel-related Usenet newsgroups also exist, such as rec.travel.fly, which revolves around air travel, and rec.travel.marketplace, for people seeking accommodations and other travel information and services. These newsgroups vary widely in the quality of information they offer, but you never know what you might find. Some of the online services, such as America Online and CompuServe, offer gateways to newsgroups.

## America Online: Savvy Travel for the MTV Generation

CompuServe may be the most comprehensive online system for travel, but America Online is the service of choice when it comes to travel information for the younger generation. While CompuServe has a more conservative bent, catering more to the business traveler and older consumer, America Online, with its easy-to-use interface, multitude of busy "chat" rooms that resemble 900 party lines, catchy graphics, and tons of information geared toward the active and youthful, is clearly made for the youth of today. AOL's travel section is designed to appeal to younger, more adventurous travelers. Here's a sample of what you'll find:

> *AOL's travel section is designed to appeal to younger, more adventurous travelers.*

- ➡ A wide selection of adventure-oriented magazines, including *Backpacker's* magazine, *Bicycler* magazine, *Flying* magazine, *Travel Holiday* magazine, and *National Geographic*

- ➡ A selection of travel books online from such companies as Michelin Green and Lonely Planet (keyword: BOOKSTORE)

- ➡ *Bed & Breakfast USA* (Keyword: BED & BREAKFAST), a useful B&B database put out by the Tourist House Association. Bed & Breakfast USA includes not only a wide selection of B&Bs in the U.S. and Canada, but also favorite B&B recipes, wheelchair-accessible B&Bs, and "how to start your own B&B." The database allows you to search using keywords describing your preferences.

- ➡ *Outdoor Adventure Online* (Keyword: OAO), a service available only to America Online users, designed to provide outdoor enthusiasts with all the information they need to plan an outdoor adventure. OAO provides access to several categories of travel data, including

- ➡ Guides and Tours, which provides data on outdoor guide services and outfitters, both in the U.S. and other countries. Interested in finding out more about llama trekking companies? This is your best bet.

- ➡ Destinations & Resorts, which profiles national parks, ski resorts, ranches, dive sites, fishing and sailing areas, and much more. These profiles also highlight the best trails throughout North America for hikers and mountain bikers.

- ➡ Ultimate Adventures, which reviews hundreds of adventure holidays around the world, and includes the best travel services to use along with itineraries and pricing.

- ➡ Outdoor Products, which reviews a variety of outdoor gear. OAO has plans to include a classified section for used gear.

- ➡ Adventure Newsline, a frequently updated news section focusing on the outdoors. Includes information on ski conditions, trip discounts, and more.

- ➡ Travel Library, which contains 600 reviews of travel guidebooks and travel-related manuals, and also includes a database of maps.

- ➡ Going Places, a regular column that provides information on saving money on airfares, hot spots, visa, passport, and insurance information, and extensive vehicle and transport information.

OAO also includes a message board, an event calendar that allows you to search for events by type of activity or location, and a download library that contains a variety of useful travel files, including some on discount travel clubs.

- ➡ *Pictures of the World*, a forum on travel photography.

- ➡ *Travelers' Corner*, a service that offers information about exotic destinations and tours as well as travel profiles on various destinations.

- ➡ *Travelers' Advantage*, a service that offers (for a fee) discounts on hotels, car rentals, and vacation packages.

**Outdoor Adventure Online shows you how to rough it in style**

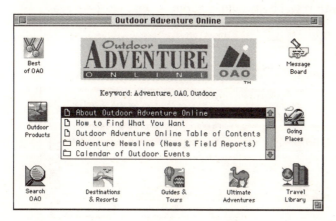

AOL's Travel Forum includes many articles and discussions of interest to the young and spontaneous traveler. You can, for example, learn how to travel cheaply as an air courier; learn about booking travel through consolidators—cut-rate travel agencies offering last-minute deals on air travel and lodging; learn about cheap airfare strategies, discount airlines, discount hotel-booking services, and more. You can also purchase online a wide variety of travel-related books at a 10 to 20 percent discount. In the forum's File Library, you'll find a huge selection of personal travel logs, road trip suggestions, tips from travel agents, and discussions and information about subjects ranging from teaching jobs in Japan to the police force in Belgium. You'll also find updated information about Eurail and Britrail. The Travel cafe, while not nearly as crowded as the MTV chat rooms, are friendly and unintimidating, and they allow you to communicate in real time instead of waiting for hours for a response.

# BBSs: You Never Know What You Might Find

Bulletin board systems—most of which consist simply of a terminal with the appropriate software and a benevolent soul who keeps track of the zillions of files that pass through it regularly—are a good deal for the bargain hunter for a

### Excuse me...is this seat taken?

America Online's Travel Cafe, located in the Travel Forum, is often filled with travel buffs talking about—what else?—travel.

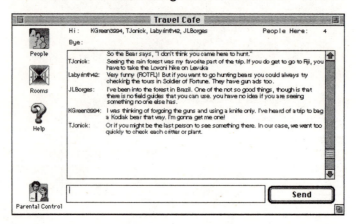

few reasons. First of all, many BBSs are free except for long-distance charges, and many of those that aren't allow you a trial period to check out the system for free. Second, you don't need to be hooked up to an online system or the Internet to dial up a BBS—all you need is a computer, a modem, and a phone line. Third, there are thousands of BBSs across the country—and around the world, if you don't mind the giant phone bill dialing them up will incur—and new ones are cropping up all the time.

However, the unstable nature of bulletin boards also makes some of them a somewhat unreliable source of information. You can find lists of BBSs online—for example, there's a frequently updated and comprehensive listing in ZiffNet's *Computer Shopper* section—but BBSs are always changing hands, changing formats, and going under. You just never know.

Here are a few travel-oriented bulletin boards that may offer some travel tips to the bargain hunter:

| Access America | (918) 747-2542 |
| Europe through the Back Door | (206) 771-1902 |

| National Park Service | (215) 597-2710 |
| --- | --- |
| Travel Connection | (415) 691-0954 |
| Travel Info Net | (519) 428-9287 |

Check out *Boardwatch* magazine, any of the BBS-oriented newsgroups, or Ziff-Net for a more complete listing.

### Looking for a real bargain? Do your homework.

Finding the best travel bargains may require a bit more work than simply logging on to Eaasy Sabre and choosing the Bargain Finder option. The Internet, bulletin boards, and online services offer a wealth of information about bargain travel, but you may have to research your destination and even (gasp!) make your reservations by phone to get the best deals.

### ➔ *Finding Rock-Bottom Rates*

While reservations services such as Eaasy Sabre offer bargain options for airplane and hotel reservations, you may find better deals by doing your research on computer and following up by phone. For example, you can find a wellspring of information online about consolidators. Airlines sell tickets to consolidators at a great discount for flights that are underbooked, and (ideally) consolidators pass this savings on to you. Many online services offer advice about which consolidators to use and which to avoid, along with lists of phone numbers. For cheap air travel in Europe, search the travel archives for information about air passes to your destination country, which are offered at a discounted rate through the country's tourist board. Also, some online services offer incentive packages for various forms of travel—for example, America Online offers a discount on Eurail passes to its users—but in most cases, you have to make the reservations yourself.

## Arranging a Home Swap Online

Home swapping is becoming an increasingly popular way to save money on lodging and spend a more substantial amount of time exploring one city or area. By swapping homes with someone overseas or across the country for a few weeks or months, you can relax and enjoy the comforts of home—though not your home—in a foreign land.

> *By swapping homes with someone overseas or across the country for a few weeks or months, you can relax and enjoy the comforts of home—though not your home—in a foreign land.*

Of course, home swapping is not without its obvious disadvantages. First of all, you have no way of really knowing if it's an even trade; no amount of pictures or descriptions will tell you everything about your prospective home. And some people are uncomfortable with strangers living unsupervised in their homes.

If you're intrigued by the idea of arranging a home swap, there are several resources online that can help you find out more about it. Travel libraries in the online services contain many discussions about the merits and disadvantages of swapping, as well as personal accounts of good and bad experiences. You can try to arrange a home swap yourself by posting a message on a forum with your request and a description of your home and region. A more organized route is the Home Exchange BBS, a service that devotes itself exclusively to arranging home swaps. You can access this BBS at (407) 869-5956.

### Home Exchange helps you find your home away from home

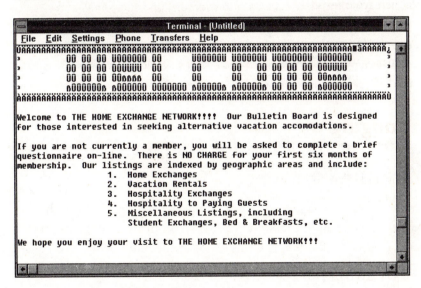

## ➜ Tracking Your Frequent Flyer Miles

It goes without saying that you can't get a better bargain than a free ride. And if you're a frequent flyer, you may be missing a valuable opportunity to cash in on that free ride if you don't take advantage of airlines' frequent flyer programs. These programs vary greatly from airline to airline, but if you play your cards right you'll have your free ticket to paradise in hand after you've flown the designated number of miles.

However, if you use several airlines in your travels, keeping track of all your frequent flyer miles can be a daunting task. And that's where frequent flyer shareware comes in. These databases can keep track of monthly statements, monitor your awards, and even dial up the airlines automatically to request the awards when you've earned the miles. An abundance of frequent flyer software can be found in the software and travel libraries of any online service and on many BBSs—and since it's shareware, you can try it for free before registering it.

## Let's Go: The Popular Budget Guide Goes Multimedia

While trip-mapping and language-learning software has saturated the multimedia market, there's still not too much out there in the way of budget travel-related titles. This will undoubtedly change soon as the multimedia market continues to explode. Until then, there's Compton's *Let's Go: The Budget Guide to Europe*, a multimedia CD-ROM based on the book of the same name. Written by students at Harvard University, the *Let's Go* guidebook has long been considered by many to be a necessity for cheap travel around Europe.

The CD, which costs around $40, is an elegantly designed multimedia version of the guidebook. And, like the guidebook, it is updated yearly. You can hear commonly used phrases spoken in French, Italian, German, and Spanish, as well as the national anthems of most European countries. You can see photos and narrated video clips of a wide variety of destinations. Also included are country profiles; an interactive atlas; city and area maps; a comprehensive phone book; transportation, restaurant, and lodging data; and cultural information. There's even a dictionary included that shows you the definition of any word when you double-click on it. In fact, there's so much information here that it may take a few minutes to find exactly what you're looking for. Fortunately, the Idea Search option lets you search the whole CD by a word or phrase. Or you can choose the easy path and take the photo tour of Europe.

 **Let's Go: A comprehensive travel guide with a pretty face**

However, beautiful and chock-full of information though it may be, *Let's Go* does have two shortcomings. First of all, if you're looking for that out-of-the-way bistro in a back alley of Paris, you may be out of luck. Though intended for students and other young travelers, the CD, like the book, sticks to the mainstream and doesn't offer too many personal viewpoints. Second, no CD can truly take the place of a real guidebook. Since you can't take it with you when you go, it forces you to plan your trip completely before you go or take reams of computer paper along. And completely planning out a low-budget trip ahead of time often simply isn't possible (and some would say it's not nearly as fun, either). For example, most youth hostels book rooms daily on a first-come, first-served basis; and today's hole-in-the-wall, gourmet eatery may be out of business tomorrow. So chances are at some point you'll get stuck with a disconnected phone number, an abandoned hostel or restaurant, or a change in the train schedule that forces you to fly by the seat of your pants, so to speak.

So, for doing research about European destinations—history, culture, linguistics, tourist attractions, places to visit, and so on—and for learning all you need to know before you embark on your journey, this beautifully crafted package is a great idea. But it won't take the place of an old-fashioned guidebook unless you plan to bring your CD player with you on your trip. (For more information, call Compton's NewMedia at (619) 929-2500.)

Kelly Green is an editor at Ziff-Davis Press. In her spare time, she freelances as a travel writer and editor.

# 7 | *Staying* Close to **Home**

**A** few years ago, anyone who wanted to get the inside scoop on local entertainment options—such as a particular big-screen movie or a restaurant in a specific area—had only a couple of very well-defined options. For starters, they could seek out the printed reviews of Hollywood's most recently released films, and perhaps a popular dining spot or two, in the local daily newspapers. (In most cities, these usually appear just once a week, perhaps on Fridays, in a newspaper's entertainment section.) If for some reason that proved insufficient, they could then seek out a regional magazine or weekly newspaper that offered essentially the same information in lengthy alphabetized listings that often contained an abbreviated form of the typical daily newspaper review. Either way, the choices were usually somewhat limited, always subject to a single writer's or editor's opinion, rarely altered after their original publication, and never exactly on hand when the average consumer really needed them most.

Like many such matters, however, the availability and depth of this type of local entertainment news has been dramatically broadened by the appearance and proliferation of the personal computer. In fact, thanks to computers, today's movie buff and restaurant-goer now often has as much information at his or her fingertips as the average professional media reviewer—and can access that information whenever it is convenient, right from the comforts of home. Sometimes, special software or a subscription to a commercial online service is required. Other times, all that may be needed is a modem to connect your computer to a free or low-cost information provider.

Once you know how to do it, there are numerous advantages to using a computer to sort through the listings and reviews available for movies and restaurants (as well as theater performances, musical concerts, and various other live entertainment events). For one thing, you can usually tap into one of several different databases and thus consider a wider array of opinions than a typical printed source is likely to offer. For another, you can often define your search by parameters that you determine—such as action movies with a specific star or romantic restaurants in a particular part of town. For yet another, you can easily print out the results of your search and then walk away from your computer with all of the little details (hours, prices, acceptable credit cards, addresses, phone numbers, and sometimes even a map of the exact location) that you'll need for a terrific night on the town. And, perhaps most significantly, details such as these can usually be obtained for entertainment options right in your backyard as well as for many cities across the country and around the world.

There are, of course, some cautions and even a few disadvantages to be aware of when using computers to obtain localized entertainment information of this kind:

> Always consider the source when gathering details from any public on-line forum. (The people who are posting the reviews, for instance, could be directly associated with the production or the establishment that they are discussing—or with one of its competitors—and so may not be entirely honest or unbiased in their assessments.)

> The costs that can be amassed when searching a commercial online database may far exceed the benefits, as opposed to obtaining the same or similar information from a daily newspaper or regional magazine.

> Some commercial software and CD-ROM products are so incomplete or outdated that they render the information either completely worthless or substantially useless.

Such potential drawbacks, though, are definitely minor when compared with the vast wealth of entertainment data that can be accessed by means of a personal computer—and the ease with which such critical and informative details can be obtained.

## What's Available, and What's Needed to Use It

As personal computers become more commonplace in the home—and the number equipped with modems and CD-ROM drives continues to grow—the number of products and services aimed at providing localized entertainment information has also mushroomed. Just a year ago, the available options were far more limited than they are today. Tomorrow, of course, they will be even greater.

Perhaps the fastest-growing and most popular source of this type of information is the online service, which is accessible to anyone with a computer and a modem. Generally open 24 hours a day, seven days a week, these electronic gathering places can regularly provide you with a convenient place to find out what others—professional reviewers and regular consumers alike—think about movies, places to eat out, and various other ways to spend a night on the town. Many give you the opportunity to speak back to the reviewers, publicly or privately, and post your own opinions on the restaurants you have visited and the films you have seen. Some also make available a wide amount of related information, ranging from the recipe of an eatery's most popular dish to a biography of a movie's stars, complete with photographs.

Nearly all of the major commercial online services, such as America Online, CompuServe, and Prodigy, offer either searchable databases with reviews and listings or public forums where members can share their own thoughts and opinions. Several also have areas filled with related information, and some even bring relevant personalities online—such as a famous chef or a film director—to answer questions posed directly by the online public. It is simple to find and join these services, and relatively easy to access their entertainment information. Some people, however, may find that their cost is too steep to warrant regular use of this type.

A similar but usually much less expensive alternative is the electronic bulletin board service, or BBS, which is also accessible to everyone with a modem-equipped computer. Since BBSs are often focused on a specific geographical area or a particular topic, they can sometimes provide even more timely and detailed information on various entertainment possibilities than a larger commercial service offering similar features can. Since many are operated on a noncommercial basis by hobbyists, or as an adjunct service by print publications such as daily newspapers and regional magazines that have already compiled the data for use in another form, they are often free to local callers or available for a very minimal charge. Because of these very reasons, though, BBSs can also be initially more difficult to locate and somewhat more difficult to use efficiently.

A third related possibility is the enormous but comparatively unstructured global computer network known as the Internet. A modem-equipped computer and a subscription to a service provider are again required for access, which can open up a vast world of opportunities for the adept user savvy in the ways of the Net. Advantages include a variety of freewheeling and often passionate discussions on everything from a movie's plot to the merits of its marketing program, and the nuances of a restaurant's menu as well as its use of

### Find out more about your favorite restaurant—online!

Online services provide meeting places that allow users to discuss such divergent topics as hot new movies and favorite recipes of restaurants around the world. Who knows, you might even be able to ask your favorite chef "in person!"

a particular ingredient. Among the disadvantages is the relatively unfriendly navigational interface; in other words, at least in comparison to the commercial online services and most BBSs, on the Net it is far more difficult to find what you want.

A final option is software or CD-ROM products created expressly for this purpose, or for a closely related one. A good example of this is trip planning software, which contains excellent information on a given area's dining and nightlife possibilities as well as the routes that will get you there. (See Chapter 3 for more information.) These products vary greatly in both list price and practicality, with CD-ROMs generally costing the most but also offering the most detailed information on a topic or a geographical region by virtue of their far larger storage capabilities. A major advantage to the software route is the fact that no special equipment is needed for the disk versions—CD-ROMs, of course, require a CD-ROM drive—as well as their relatively low one-time cost and their availability for all manner of computers in all of today's common platforms (Macintosh, Windows, and DOS).

One major disadvantage of both entertainment software and CD-ROMs is the fact that information contained on them is static and can quickly become outdated. Another is that they are usually available for only the largest cities and often contain information on just the biggest movies and stars. Some publishers try to ameliorate this problem by offering yearly updates of their software to registered users at reduced prices.

## Finding Entertainment Information Online

Because of their extensive media and marketing campaigns, it has become increasingly difficult these days to escape the reach of the major commercial online services. All of them advertise extensively in computer publications and even a variety of general-interest magazines. Most will ship free access software to anyone who requests it and provide them with a free trial subscription period. Some, like America Online, package free startup disks with related products. Others, like Prodigy, come bundled with the software preloaded into new computers.

Once you subscribe, all of the various entertainment-oriented features that are offered by these online providers are yours for the taking—for a price, of course. To access what they have to offer at any time of the day or night, you simply use your modem to dial into the service (usually a simple point-and-click procedure with today's machines) and sign on (usually handled automatically with information you have previously provided). Then, by using simple commands that are unique to that service, you can move about or navigate its different areas to find the specific information that you want. Most of the services offer some sort of an online directory—or at least a way to find general categories of information once you've logged on—as well as a printed version of their service capabilities. (Once online, for instance, you can usually find out which areas contain information on *restaurants* or *cinema*, and then transfer directly to those areas.)

A few of the very best avenues for obtaining online entertainment information are described below.

> *If it's information on rock 'n' roll that you're after, and you want to trade quips and opinions with like-minded fans, enter the RockLink department (keyword: ROCKLINK) or the MTV Forum.*

America Online offers a few areas specifically geared toward those seeking details or conversation on outside entertainment. To enter any of these departments, select Keyword from the Go To menu or press the Ctrl and K keys at the same time. Then enter a keyword and click on the OK button. Hourly charges accrue after a subscriber's monthly hourly allotment has been used up.

Through AOL, you can access current Hollywood news and film reviews (keyword: MOVIES). If it's information on rock 'n' roll that you're after, and you want to trade quips and opinions with like-minded fans, enter the RockLink department (keyword: ROCKLINK) or the MTV Forum. A growing but still limited number of geographical areas, such as Chicago, have been given their own online areas (keyword: COL). In addition, AOL has compiled the electronic world's largest collection of online publications; many of these offer useful but more generalized information. To get major cinematic stories or current movie reviews with a national perspective, for instance, try the cyberspace editions of *USA Today* (keyword: USATODAY) or *Time* magazine (keyword: TIME).

To find other sources of related information, search the Directory of Services by pulling down the Go To menu, select Search the Directory of Services, and then type in a word or two describing the features in which you are interested (such as *Food* or *Broadway Theater*). A list and descriptions of all the related departments will appear on your screen.

CompuServe has a slew of Forums and databases dedicated to the pursuit of leisure. To access a particular area from anywhere within CompuServe, use the GO command—either from the pull-down menu at the top of the screen or by means of the stoplight-like icon on any of its graphical navigation systems—followed by the service's specific designation. CompuServe's pricing structure is more complicated than any of the other services; most of the areas with entertainment information carry hourly charges (designated by a plus sign), and some have additional surcharges as well. For that reason it is usually best to determine what you want before logging on and then download the information for later reading offline. (Almost everything can be "checked off" with a mouse click and then sent to your File Cabinet or another designated file on your hard drive for leisurely—and less costly—study.)

Two of the service's best features in this area, however, are included in CompuServe's Basic Services and do not garner any additional charges beyond your monthly subscription fee. One is Roger Ebert's Movie Reviews (GO EBERT). This searchable database of 20 years worth of the Pulitzer Prize-winning journalist's writings includes his "Most Recent Movie Reviews" as well as older reviews, essays, a humorous glossary of movie terms, various top ten lists, video reviews, and a suggestion box that can be used to contact him directly. As with all areas on this service, you highlight the menu option you want with a single mouse click and then click the GO button directly above the menu. A secondary menu will appear in the same space, and you click on the review or list that you want and then click the GO button once more.

### *Access Roger Ebert's movie reviews through CompuServe*

As part of its Basic Services, CompuServe offers you a direct line to Roger Ebert and his prizewinning movie reviews. Browse reviews of old and new titles, Roger's top ten, and more; or contact him directly through the suggestion box.

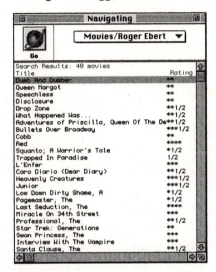

The other useful option in Basic Services—this time in the dining-out category—is the Zagat Survey (GO ZAGAT) by Eugene and Nina Zagat. This online version of the couple's popular regional restaurant guide covers most major U.S. cities (like Atlanta, Kansas City, and Portland) and regions (like the Hawaiian Islands and Philadelphia/Atlantic City/Bucks County/South New Jersey/Wilmington). Reviews, updated annually, can be searched by

**1.** Selecting the city or region that interests you

**2.** Following the on-screen prompts to narrow your search

**3.** Selecting either the name of the restaurant, neighborhood, type of cuisine, or price range in which you are interested.

**Find reviews for restaurants around the country with the Zagat Survey**

A number of related options, all accruing hourly charges, are also available on CompuServe. Among the most useful is the Magill's Survey of Cinema (GO MAGILL), which is a database containing descriptions of most major films from 1902 to the present; available information includes a film's title, release date, running time, country of release, cast and credits, production studio, rating, annotation on reviews, and plot summary. (Along with the hourly charges, the cost for this service is $2 for each 10 titles located.) In addition, many of the magazines and newspapers available through CompuServe (GO NEWSUSA) contain restaurant and movie reviews that can be accessed through searchable databases; the cost includes a surcharge as well as hourly charges.

Prodigy is a family-friendly online service that offers a variety of entertainment functions and several different pricing plans. Most areas can be accessed by using its JUMP command; to use it, press J and Enter simultaneously, then type in the JUMP word for the service you want and press Enter once more. A complete list of available JUMP words can be obtained by scrolling down the JUMP word window at the top of the screen and then clicking on INDEX.

One excellent entertainment-oriented service on Prodigy is the Mobil Travel Guide (JUMP MOBIL GUIDE), the online version of the popular guidebook of the same name. It features Mobil's highly regarded ratings of restaurants and lodgings in 53 U.S. cities, along with related information on local sports and recreation and other entertainment options. After you reach the main menu, select the city index to find the specific details that you require. For even more useful data, you can use this along with the service's Metro Find (JUMP METRO FIND). This allows you to call up a variety of city guides produced by Prodigy users, as well as Zagat restaurant reviews. Additionally, you can access Magill's Survey of Cinema (JUMP MOVIE GUIDE). Its main menu tells you how to easily find films by title, genre, star, director, or year.

Prodigy also offers an expanded online version of Worldview Systems's city guide (JUMP WORLDVIEW), the seven-year-old service from Random House/Fodor's Travel Publications that allows you to create a customized listing of events and local attractions—ranging from dining choices and nightlife to spectator sporting events and one-time exhibitions—for a specific city during a specific time period for a fee of $4.95. Over 130 destinations are available across the U.S. and around the world.

## Finding Entertainment Information through Electronic Bulletin Boards

BBSs, or local electronic bulletin boards, offer many of the same types of services as the commercial online services—but for free or at a very low cost. If you can find one that is located in your area, even the call may be free; otherwise, long-distance calling charges may be assessed. Only a few central listings of BBS services are completely accurate and always up-to-date, however, so you may have to do some initial digging to uncover a board that concentrates on the area or topics that strike your fancy. One solid source of reliable information is Boardwatch magazine, which periodically runs listings of BBSs in various locales around the U.S. and usually carries classified ads that describe boards geared to a variety of special interests.

Here are a few examples of useful and free regional BBSs.

*LA Online* is an excellent example of a dining-and-nightlife BBS that is accessible for free, after any applicable long-distance calling charges, to anyone with a computer and modem. Operated by the publishers of several Los Angeles newspapers, it offers southern California calendars of events, restaurant listings and reviews, movie times and reviews, and more. After you connect, its main menu gives you easy-to-follow instructions for accessing various types of entertainment information; subsequent menus offer simple routes to its various reviews, listings, stories, and additional information sources. Most data can be obtained by pressing the number or letter directly adjacent to your choice and then pressing Enter.

### Find out about L.A. nightlife—and more!—from LA Online

The LA Online bulletin board includes not only constantly updated calendars of events for the Los Angeles area, but also lets you see articles appearing in local-area weeklies and newspapers.

```
[    Enter Option # or press X to exit -> 1

L.A. READER On-line Edition, Nov 18 to Nov 24                    MAIN MENU
---------------------------------------- . ----------------------------------
| To pull up the L.A. Reader in color :
| with multiple fonts, buttons & cool : The Beat and How to Get It (Again)
| graphics, purchase LA.EXE Version 2.: Go-Go's Talk Dirty and Influence
| To order type GO GRAPHICS.          : People
*-----------------------------------: By Erik Himmelsbach
SECTIONS:                            : "You look familiar," Kathy Valentine
StraightDope....A                    : says as she scavenges through the
CitySide........B  Rock & Pop......M : remains of what were once many bags o
Classifieds.....C  Jazz...........N : bagels. "We didn't have our way with
Weird News......D  Comedy.........P : you on the bus, did we?" Nope, it
Leaders.........E  Acoustic.......Q : wasn't me. But Valentine's confusion
Restaurants.....H  Concerts.......R : is understandable. After all, those o
Books...........I  Classical......S : us "lucky" enough to have viewed a
Art World.......J  The Movies.....T : certain infamous underground video, i
Seven Days......K  Movie Times....W : which Valentine and a dazed 'n'
Theater.........L  EXIT...........X : confused Belinda Carlisle toy with a
                                                         COVER STORY [Page 2

Enter Selection -> █
```

*Colorado TravelBank* is another example of a free BBS that offers a plethora of localized entertainment data. A modem-accessible source of year-round travel and recreation information for Colorado's mountain resorts as well as its major cities, TravelBank is also a simple menu-driven guide to local dining, night spots, and other entertainment options. After reaching its main menu, hit the asterisk key (*) to get to the Lodging, Dining, Nite-Life & Shopping menu; then, an additional menu will appear with detailed instructions on how to choose from among a series of codes to find the specific information you want. If you seek an Italian restaurant in Denver, for example, you type DEN, DIN, ITL and then hit Return. A third menu will appear on the screen with choices that meet this criteria; each has a phone number alongside the restaurant's name, and some have an adjacent code number that can then be entered for even more information.

➡️ **Explore Colorado's entertainment options through Colorado TravelBank**

Colorado TravelBank lets you search for detailed information about your entertainment and dining options. Want to find an Italian restaurant in Denver? No problem.

```
Type search key or <CR> to quit: Den, Itl
                +------------------------------------------+
   I            |    Welcome to The Colorado TravelBank's   |
                |        Dining, Nite-Life & Shopping       |
                |              Data-Base                     |
                +------------------------------------------+
Extended
Information
ID.-#     NAME/ Phone Number        TYPE       LOCATION(S)/ CODES
==================================================================
D218  Gabriel's, 303-688-2323       DINE   DEN ITL PRICE
D130  Mike Berardi's, 303-399-8800  DINE   DEN ITL MEX  Juanita's Uptown
      Fratelli's Rest. & Bakery     DINE   DEN ITL PZZA
D221  Bonnie Brae Tavern, 303-777-2262  DINE   DEN ITL PZZA
D222  Falcone's, 303-777-0707       DINE   DEN ITL
      Sfuzzi, 303-321-4700          DINE   DEN ITL

Type Record ID you want more on or <CR> to exit:
```

# Exploring Entertainment Options through the Internet

The Internet is perhaps the most often discussed of all online options, but for many novices (and even some experienced computer users) it can prove to be a navigational nightmare. If you know how to use it, and if you know what you are looking for, however, it can provide many solid options for entertainment information. To surf the Net, you must again have a modem-equipped computer and Internet access (offered by many providers, including several commercial online services and numerous BBSs). Worldview Systems, described above, is also accessible on the Internet by typing http://gnn.com/gnn/bus/wview/index.html. Highlights of all available destinations, one monthly featured destination in its entirety, and the ability to request customized itineraries can be obtained by following the online instructions that appear on your screen. Additionally, there are a wide variety of *newsgroups*, or online discussion forums, that concentrate on entertainment topics. Try rec.food.restaurants for chat about individual sites as well as related topics such as smoking versus nonsmoking policies; and rec.arts.movies.reviews for a variety of reviews on current fare.

 ### Browse the rec.arts.movies.reviews newsgroup via CompuServe

You can access some, though not all, Internet services through the commercial online services. For example, newsgroups such as this one can be accessed through CompuServe by using the GO word INTERNET and choosing Usenet newsgroups from the list.

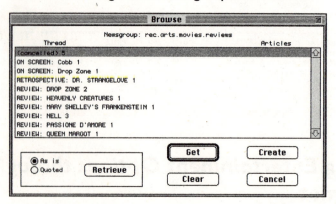

## *Software for After Hours*

While there are some drawbacks to software-based entertainment products—primarily the fact that they become somewhat outdated the moment they are released—their cost and ease of use, not to mention the ability they give you to leisurely browse their contents, make them more than worthwhile for many applications. Using them to gather information on established restaurants, for example, is efficient and fun; just don't forget to call ahead and make sure the information (particularly hours of operation) is still accurate. For movies, they can't tell you anything about the film opening this coming weekend, but they are great sources of background information and can't be beat for help in choosing a video rental.

The number of titles available in this area expands faster than the information they attempt to capture. To keep updated, read computer magazines for newly reviewed products and ask your local software dealer for advice. If you have a computer with a CD-ROM drive, these products are often best because they contain far more information than their cousins on floppy disks and also can combine sound and full-motion video with text. Some CDs, though, are little more than electronic versions of existing books and do nothing more than their printed predecessors—at a much higher price.

> *To keep updated, read computer magazines for newly reviewed products and ask your local software dealer for advice.*

One product that does do what it promises is *Taxi*, available on 3.5-inch floppies or CD-ROM. This excellent trip-planning software covers about 20 major U.S. cities such as New York, Chicago, Los Angeles, Washington, D.C., San Francisco, Boston, Philadelphia, Seattle, and Phoenix. Using a sophisticated mapping database for each city—combined with Zagat restaurant and hotel ratings and reviews—it allows you to locate an eatery by various criteria such as location, price range, cuisine, or even special features (like "romantic," "young children," "entertainment," and "late night"). These categories can be combined, for example, by asking for a review of all "romantic Japanese restaurants downtown" and then locating them precisely on a city map; the software can then be instructed to give you specific directions from, say, your hotel to the restaurant. The software is easy to use, with clearly marked pop-up menus and simple point-and-click technology. Other trip-planning software, such as AAA Trip Planner and DeLorme Map 'n' Go (see Chapter 3) are good sources of information about regional activities as well as for mapping out trips. (Check out the AAA Trip Planner on the CD accompanying this book.)

### ➡ *Taxi trip planning software*

Easy-to-use, detailed, and sophisticated, Taxi lets you choose your destination by various criteria and then locate it precisely on a city map.

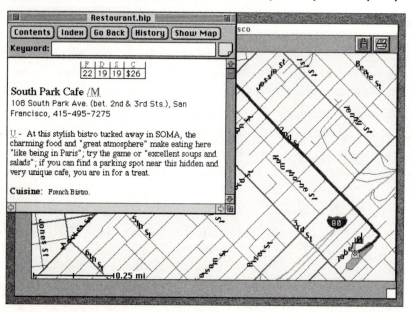

Two other guidebook-type CD-ROM products worth considering are *Washington, D.C. at Its Best* and *New York at Its Best*, both variations on printed books written by Robert S. Kane. The former contains information on 130 restaurants and 70 hotels; the latter has over 200 restaurants and 80 hotels. Both also feature museums, historic sites, and other attractions. Point-and-click technology allows you to easily search for a restaurant by name, cuisine, location, or price range. Full reviews of selected eateries include descriptions of the decor as well

as selected menu items. A few street maps are offered, although they are somewhat fuzzy and only in black-and-white. There is also an audio button that,
when clicked, "reads" the on-screen text. It is computer generated, however, and
very difficult to understand.

### Washington, D.C. at its Best
Offering information on 130 restaurants, 70 hotels, and many other attractions, Washington, D.C. at its Best is one of the most comprehensive single-city CDs around.

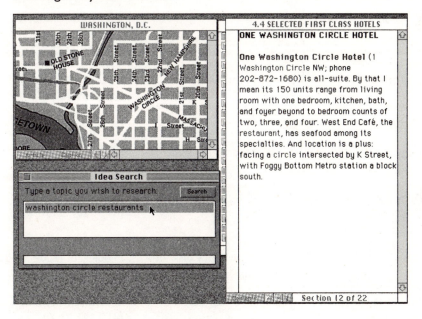

Movie-wise, software products are far more limited. *Cinemania '95* may be the
very best, offering a variety of ways to locate and recall information on your favorite actor, director, or film. The CD-ROM also includes many actual video
clips as well as numerous still photos from assorted movies. *Mega Movie Guide
3.0*, another CD-ROM, also contains plenty of film clips and "trailers" from some
of the best-loved movies of all time. Additional features include 42,000 movie reviews, a listing of all major Academy Award winners and nominees, bibliogra-
phies, still photos, a section on Greatest Hits of the Decade, and more.

## Entertainment Products and Their Manufacturers

| Product Name | Product Description | Vendor Information |
|---|---|---|
| AAA Trip Planner | CD-ROM for Windows | Compton's NewMedia (619-929-2500) |
| *Boardwatch* magazine | Trade publication covering the BBS industry | Boardwatch (303-973-6038) |
| Cinemania '95 | CD-ROM for Windows, DOS, Mac | Microsoft (800-426-9400) |
| Colorado TravelBank | BBS | Colorado TravelBank (303-671-7669 modem, 303-320-8550 voice) |
| DeLorme Map 'n' Go | CD-ROM for Windows | DeLorme Mapping (207-865-1234) |
| LA Online | BBS | LA Online (310-445-0633) |
| Mega Movie Guide 3.0 | CD-ROM for Windows | InfoBusiness Inc. (800-657-5300) |
| New York at Its Best, Washington, D.C. at Its Best | CD-ROM for Windows, DOS, Mac | Compton's New Media (619-929-2500) |
| Taxi | CD-ROM or floppy disk for IBM-compatibles and Macintosh | Middlegate (800-439-8294) |
| Worldview Systems | Customized service | Worldview Systems Corp. (415-391-7100) |

Howard Rothman is a Colorado-based writer who specializes in travel, business, and computer topics. He is the author of six books and more than 1,000 articles for 70 magazines and newspapers. His latest book, *A Whole New Ballgame: The Evolution of America's National Pastime,* will be released by PendletonClay Publishers in spring of 1995.

# *Appendix:* How to Use the CD-ROM

The CD-ROM accompanying this book contains a variety of multimedia demos, shareware products, an online connection to CompuServe via WinCIM, information about other Ziff-Davis Press books, and more. Here's what you need to use the CD:

- ✔ IBM-compatible PC
- ✔ 386DX-33 (486DX-33 or faster recommended)
- ✔ 4MB RAM (minimum)
- ✔ 4MB available on hard drive
- ✔ Super VGA adapter (supporting 640X480 resolution and 256 colors) highly recommended
- ✔ Microsoft mouse or 100% compatible
- ✔ Microsoft Windows 3.1 or higher
- ✔ MS-DOS 3.0 or higher
- ✔ Single-speed CD-ROM drive (double-speed recommended)

## Installing the CD

To install the Smart Travel icon on your desktop in the Ziff-Davis Press program group, go to File Manager and double-click on INSTALL.EXE. To run the CD directly without installing it on the desktop, double-click on RUN_ME.EXE in File Manager. Don't forget to read the READ ME file that appears in the program group where you installed the CD.

## Accessing Files on the CD

To view any of the travel demos—Lyric Language, PictureIt!, or AAA Trip Planner—simply click on Travel Demos on the main screen and then click on the demo you wish to see. These demos run directly from the CD.

**NOTE** When you run PictureIt! and AAA Trip Planner, a dialog box for Director Player 4.0 may appear with the message *Script error: X Lib file not found.* If this happens, simply press Continue; this does not in any way interfere with the performance of the demos.

To access any of the files in the Shareware...and More! section, you must download them to your computer. First click on Shareware...and More! on the main screen. A list of files will appear. You can either highlight the file in the list that you wish to install and press the Install icon or double-click on the file. Doing this brings up a dialog box showing the default download settings. Unless you specify otherwise, the files will be downloaded to your C drive and placed in a directory called ZDPTRAVEL. Each downloaded program will be placed in its own file within this directory.

Here's what you should see in the list:

TRAVEL-MATE 3.2, a DOS shareware program for the frequent traveler. Includes many useful tools, utilities, and travel information. Requires a hard drive with 3.3 megabytes free and DOS 3.3 or higher. If you like this program and continue to use it, be sure to register it. (To install after downloading, go to the TRAVMATE folder in the ZDPTRAVEL directory and double-click on TRAVMATE.EXE.)

**NOTE** TRAVEL-MATE requires a sizable chunk of memory; if it doesn't run in Windows, try running it directly from DOS.

Travel Bag 2.0, a freeware program for Windows that shows hotel, airline, and auto rental 800 numbers; emergency numbers; and Las Vegas hotel and show information, all in a colorful, easy-to-read format. (To install after downloading, go to the TRAVBAG folder in the ZDPTRAVEL directory and double-click on INSTALL.EXE.)

Auto maintenance spreadsheet in Lotus 1-2-3 Release 4, designed to track your car repairs and help you determine how much you're spending on your vehicle (see Chapter 3 for details).

*Belize First,* a sample issue of an e-zine devoted entirely to travel, life, and culture in Belize.

# Index